THE BROADCAST COMMUNICATIONS DICTIONARY

Revised and Expanded Edition

BY LINCOLN DIAMANT, F.R.S.A.

THE ANATOMY OF A TELEVISION COMMERCIAL
TELEVISION'S CLASSIC COMMERCIALS
INTRODUCTION TO ARISTOTLE'S POLITICS & POETICS
THE BATTLE OF HARLEM HEIGHTS

The Broadcast Communications Dictionary

Revised and Expanded Edition

Edited by LINCOLN DIAMANT, F.R.S.A.

Communication Arts Books

HASTINGS HOUSE, PUBLISHERS
10 East 40th Street, New York 10016

This edition is for Leon Rosenbluth.

Library of Congress Cataloging in Publication Data
Diamant, Lincoln.
    The broadcast communications dictionary.

    (Communication arts books)
    1. Broadcasting—Dictionaries. I. Title.
PN1990.4.D5   1978   384.54'01'4   77-19258
ISBN 0-8038-0788-0

Published simultaneously in Canada by
Saunders of Toronto, Ltd., Don Mills, Ontario
Printed in the United States of America

EDITOR'S INTRODUCTION
TO THE SECOND EDITION

A man accosted Dr. Johnson in the Strand and asked him the meaning of a word. Dr. Johnson replied, "Do not ASK me, Sir. Consult my book!"

Serving the world communications revolution, hundreds of thousands of workers in the United States and Great Britain have been marshaled into a host of technical disciplines that rarely overlap. When they do talk across party lines, they discover their native tongue has suddenly developed a proliferation of terms unparalleled in the history of language.

For example, verbatim from the April 11, 1977 issue of *Broadcast:*

Setting aside the loony idea currently floating around the EBU of handling U-Matic ENG at 525/NTSC on the Eurovision circuits (and presumably employing £2,000,000 standards converters to transmit the pictures produced by these £2,000 recorders in a fit of technological overkill), one answer may lie in the various image enhancing systems which were being touted at the NAB.

The first edition of this dictionary—from "AA" to "Zworykin"—defined all those terms. This second edition, striving to stay abreast of even newer developments, neologisms and swirling acronyms, has swelled the original word stock by almost 100%. "A contemporary dictionary maker," notes *The New York Times*, "runs against time. He has to. Unless he gets a move on, he can fall farther and farther behind, as his dictionary takes longer to record linguistic developments than they take to happen."

Broadcast communications are a perfect example. In this age of babbling satellites, one must first know exactly what the other fellow is *saying*, to know what he is *doing*. While hardly a substitute for a technical encyclopedia—a full discussion of only a few of these thousands of terms would require a library—this handy quick reference book is designed for everyday assistance. *Italicized cross-references* serve to underline important interrelationships, easing the way to more concise, convenient usage.

Eschewing picayunish alphabet soup, this dictionary strives to permit all who work in English-speaking broadcast communications around the world to use the same language. The international success of the first edition suggests acceptance.

In doubt? Echoing Dr. Johnson (but a bit more humbly), *"Please consult my book."*

Pondside
Ossining, New York
New Year's Day, 1978

A

AA—Advertising Association: British trade group exchanging information and establishing general policy and industry standards. Compare: *AAAA, Advertising Council, ANA, IPA, ISBA, NA(RT)B*.

AAAA—4 A's—American Association of Advertising Agencies: agency group exchanging information and establishing general policy and industry standards. Compare: *AA, Advertising Council, ANA, IPA, ISBA, NA(RT)B*.

AA (average audience) rating: percentage of *television homes* viewing average minute of national *telecast*.

A & B rolls: overlapped sections of *negative film* (or *video tape*) wound on separate *reels* to obtain *printing* (or *editing*) *dissolves* or other *optical effects*. See: *checkerboarding*. Compare: *A-roll, B-roll*.

A & B winds: *emulsion* location on either side of *16mm single-perf film base*. "A wind" (*emulsion* toward *reel* hub) is generally for *contact printing;* "B wind" (*base* toward *reel* hub) is for camera *raw stock,* projection *printing* and *optical* work.

A & R—artists and repertoire: recording corporation division handling performers and material.

A/B: as before.

ABC—American Broadcasting Companies: U.S. conglomerate

broadcasting network. See: *Hard Rock.* Also: **ABC—Audit Bureau of Circulations:** joint industry group auditing media circulation claims. Also: Australian Broadcasting Commission.

aberration: television *image* distortion, caused by *signal interference* or electron *beam* mis-*alignment.* Also: Optical *lens* malfunction.

above the line: "creative"—as distinguished from "technical"—*program* costs. Compare: *below the line.*

A-box: in Britain, multi-outlet power distribution unit.

ABS—Association of Broadcasting and Allied Staffs: labor union representing British broadcast production personnel.

absorption: retention of transmitted light within a *lens.*

A-B test: direct comparison of *component* quality through *circuit* substitution.

ABU—Asian Broadcasting Union: multi-national programming organization.

AC—alternating current: electric power supply reversing direction (polarity) at regularly recurring intervals, i.e., 60 times per second (60 *Hz*) in the U.S. (110 volts), 50 in Britain (220 volts). Compare: *DC.*

AC adapter: step-down *transformer* converting battery-operated equipment to wired power source.

Academy aperture: film *framing* standard established by American Academy of Motion Picture Arts & Sciences. See: *cutoff, reticule, safety.*

Academy leader: (non-projected) *film head* section containing visual *countdown cueing* information in "seconds" (formerly in "feet"), to standards of American Academy of Motion Picture Arts & Sciences. See: *leader.* Compare: *video leader.*

ACC: automatic *contrast* control. Also: Automatic *chrominance* control.

acceptance: local *affiliate* clearance of *network* program. Compare: *pre-emption.*

access: public availability of *cable* broadcasting time. See: *public access.*

access time: time during *video tape playback* between moment information is called for and moment delivered.

account: advertising *sponsor*. See: *client*.

account executive—AE: *agency* employee responsible for service liason with *client*.

account group: *agency* creative and management personnel servicing particular *client*.

accumulation: see *audience accumulation*.

acetate: transparent plastic sheeting used as artwork surface. Also: Individually *cut* (not *pressed*) *phonograph disk* (actually aluminum, coated with cellulose nitrate). Also: See *base*.

achromatic: without color.

acoustic: early non-electronic *disk recording* process.

acoustic feedback: see *feedback*.

acoustics: *resonance* qualities of sound *recording studio* or *stage*. See: *dead, live*.

acoustic screen: see *gobo*.

across the board: *broadcast* material scheduled at the same time each weekday. See: *strip*. Compare: *one shot, special*.

ACT—Action for Children's Television: citizen's group agitating for upgraded children's *programming*.

actinic light: visible or ultra-violet light creating chemical or electro-chemical action.

action line: "consumer assistance" programming.

action: rehearsed movement—or director's call for such movement—in front of camera. Compare: *cut*.

AC transfer: *video tape duplication* by contact between high-*coercivity master* and low-*coercivity slave* in high-frequency *AC* field. See: *bifilar, dynamic*. Compare: *STAM*.

ACTT—Association of Cinematograph, Television and Allied Technicians: labor union representing British film and television trades.

acutance: optical sharpness.

AD—assistant (or associate) director: indispensable "detail man" on set or location—before, during and after *production*. Called *production secretary* in Britain. Compare: *gopher*.

adapter: *jack, plug* or *outlet* attachment connecting dissimilar sizes.

ADC—analog-to-digital converter: equipment dissecting *analog* television *signals* into *digital transmission* form. Compare: *DAC*.

additive primaries: television's red-orange, green and blue-violet colors. In varying combinations, they produce all other colors and white. See: *primary colors, RGB, triad*.

address code—birthmark: *digital video tape retrieval* system, utilizing control *track signals*. See: *time code*.

addy: *copy* over-sophistication.

ADI—area of dominant (station) influence: *ARB* research market classification denoting the country cluster in which most *viewers* watch the "local" *stations*. Compare: *DMA*.

adjacencies: *broadcast* material immediately preceding and/or following specific *program* or *commercial*.

ad lib—ad libitum: (from Latin "at pleasure") improvise material without *rehearsal*.

advance: number of *frames* between *picture* and *synchronous* sound on *composite film print*, to accommodate projection *pullup* requirements; 20 *frames* in *35mm*, 26 *frames* in *16mm* (21 and 27 in Britain).

(advertising) agency: independent firm commissioned to handle advertising preparation for non-competitive *clients* ("15% commission, 85% confusion."—FRED ALLEN). Compare: *house agency*.

Advertising Council: semi-official U.S. group mounting "public service" propaganda compaigns with rotating *agency* assistance. Compare: *AA, AAAA, ANA, IPA, ISBA, NA(RT)B*.

advertising director (manager): corporate executive charged with advertising planning, *agency* contact and supervision. Loosely, "the *client*."

advisory: internal news service information about upcoming story. Compare: *bulletin*.

aerial—antenna: conductive device radiating or *receiving rf broadcast signals*. See: *dish*. Compare: *balloon, satellite*.

af: *audio frequency*. Compare: *rf*.

AFC: automatic *frequency* control.

affidavit: sworn *station* statement attesting broadcast of *commercial* material. Compare: *log*.

affiliate: U.S. *broadcast station* contracted to a *network* for more than 10 hours of *programming* a week. Compare: *O & O's, independent*.

AFI—American Film Institute: creative trade association. Compare: *BFI*.

AFL-CIO—American Federation of Labor–Congress of Industrial Organizations: American labor union parent body. Compare: *Trades Union Congress*.

AFM—American Federation of Musicians: music performers' union.

AFR(T)S—Armed Forces Radio (Television) Service: overseas military *broadcasting* organization.

AFTRA—American Federation of Television & Radio Artists: union covering *radio* and *video tape* performing *talent*, singers and *sound effects* artists. Compare: *SAG*.

AGB—Audits of Great Britain: market research organization: See: *JICRAR, JICTAR*. Compare: *ARB, Nielsen*.

AGC—automatic gain control: *servo circuitry* affording consistent *signal level*. Compare: *automatic gain circuit*.

agency: see *advertising agency*.

agency commission: generally 15 per cent of gross *client time* charge *billings* credited by *broadcast* medium to *agency* placing advertising.

agency of record: *agency* placing *broadcast* advertising prepared for a single corporate advertiser by several (of its) *agencies*.

agent: broadcast *talent booking* representative, usually sharing small percentage of performance fee.

agreement: in Britain, *contractual* understanding between *producer* and *talent* or trade unions.

AGVA—American Guild of Variety Artists: performers' union. Compare: *AFTRA, SAG*.

aided recall interview: in-home audience survey technique utilizing "clues" to measure recent viewing/listening (usually misses ghetto audiences).

AIR—All-India Radio: state-controlled radio network.

air—on air: actual *broadcast*.

air check: off-the-air *tape, film print* or *storyboard* copy of *commercial* for verification or competitive consideration. Compare: *line check*.

air date: scheduled day of *broadcast*.

air play: *broadcast* of musical *recording*.

air quality: produced to technical *broadcast* standards. Compare: *broadcast quality*.

airwaves: loosely, *broadcasting*.

Akai: Japanese electronics firm manufacturing *hand-held* television cameras. See: *ENG*.

ALC: automatic *level* control.

"A" lens: see *anamorphic lens*.

Alexanderson: U.S. *radio* pioneer (inventor of alternator).

alignment: correct electronic *balance*.

alignment chart: see *test pattern*.

all: in Britain, full *IBA network*.

Allen screw: flush-mounted machine screw with (hexagonal) insert head (requiring use of an Allen wrench). Compare: *Phillips screw*.

alligator: temporary *circuit* clip attachment (jaws resembling alligator). Compare: *gator grip*.

allocation—assignment: *FCC* license of specific *frequency* and *power* to a *broadcast station*. See: *call letters*.

all-news: *radio program format*.

Ally Pally—Alexandra Palace: London studios for initial *BBC* television *transmissions* (1936–1953).

alpha wrap: *video tape* wind configuration around *helical scan* drum. Compare: *omega wrap*.

alternate sponsorship: rotation of *"major"* and *"minor"* sponsorships in a *broadcast program* series, to reduce cost of advertising *exposure*.

alternative television: non-establishment television *programming*. See: *public access*.

alternator: in Britain, portable gasoline- or diesel-powered dynamo generating alternating current (*AC*).

·12·

AM—amplitude modulation: original *audio signal* transmission technique, utilizing 107 *frequencies* from 535 to 1,605 *kilohertz;* subject to atmospheric and local *signal interference.* See: *Class I, medium wave.* Compare: *FM.*

amateur: see *ham.*

ambient (light): general lighting not directed at camera subject. See: *fill light.* Compare: *key, backlight, rimlight.*

ambient (temperature): temperature of gas or liquid around equipment.

American Academy of Television Arts and Sciences: professional trade association. See: *Emmy.*

American Television & Radio Commercials Festival: annual competition honoring outstanding *broadcast commercials.* See: *Clio.*

ampere—amp: basic unit of electrical *current* strength. Compare: *ohm, volt, watt.*

Ampex: *audio* and *video tape recorder* manufacturer.

amplifier: device reproducing an enlarged version of an electronic *signal* without drawing power from the *signal.* Compare: *preamp, receiver, tuner.*

amplitude: vertical vibrations reflecting intensity of a *wave.* See: *frequency.* Compare: *wavelength.*

ANA—Association of National Advertisers: *client* group exchanging information and establishing general policy and industry standards. Compare: *AA, AAAA, Advertising Council, IPA, ISBA, NA(RT)B.*

analog: direct (usually physical) transfer of measurement to *readout signal.* Compare: *digital.* See: *ADC, DAC.*

analyze: "break down" *soundtrack* information in preparation for *animation stand* photography. See: *lead sheet.*

anamorphic lens—"A" lens: camera *lens* to compress (and projector *lens* to expand) the image, adapting standard width camera film to *widescreen* projection formats.

anastigmat: *lens* correcting horizontal/vertical plane *aberrations.*

anchorman/anchorperson: news program *MC.* Compare: *newscaster.*

anechoic chamber: "dead" room for acoustical testing.

Angenieux: French *lens* system; *zoom* widely used.

angle of acceptance—angle of view: *lens* coverage.

angle shot: non-head-on camera position.

ångström: (from the Swedish physicist) ten-billionth of a meter.

ANIKs: (from Eskimo "brother") see *TELESAT*.

animatic: (loose term for) *limited animation* technique.

animation: any photographic technique utilizing *still* subject material to give illusion of actual motion. See: *persistence of vision*.

animation board—peg board: studded drawing board (or *light box*) accurately aligning sequential animation *cels*.

animation camera—animation stand: *motion picture* camera mounted vertically over horizontal subject table (*bench*) for single-*frame exposures;* movements of both camera and table are carefully coordinated. See: *stop motion*. Called *rostrum* in Britain.

animation designer: cartoon stylist supplying key drawings—*extremes*—for *animation* sequences. See: *model sheet*. Compare: *in-betweens*.

animator—in-betweener: cartoonist working from master *key* drawings to complete a *cel* sequence.

(Lord) Annan: Parliamentary committee on British *broadcasting* directions.

announce booth: small soundproof *studio* for isolated voice *recording* on *set* or *stage*.

announcement: euphemism for *commercial*. Also: In Britain, a verbal *slate*.

announcer: program introducer, or *commercial* "pitchman." Compare: *narrator, MC*.

A(N)SI: American (National) Standards Institute *film emulsion speed rating*. Compare: *BSI, DIN*.

answer print: initial *composite* evaluation *film print* from completed *picture* and *track negative*. Called *grading print* in Britain. Compare: *release print*.

antenna—aerial: conductive device radiating or *receiving rf broadcast* signals. See: *directional, dish*. Compare: *balloon, satellite*.

antenna array: several radiating or receiving elements arranged in a system.

antenna farm: television *station antenna* grouping minimizing aerial navigation hazard.

anti-G: in Britain, *pantagraph* device suspending *luminaire* over set.

anti-halation: anti-reflective opaque *film* backing.

ANTIOPE—Acquisition Numerique et Televisualisation d'Images Organiseés en Pages d'Ecriture: French *teletext* system.

anti-skating: device reducing *phonograph pickup* skid tendency.

AP—Associated Press: subscriber news service for *broadcast stations, newspapers.* Compare: *Reuters, U.P.I.*

aperture: opening controlling amount of light (measured in *f-stops*) or electrons passing through equipment.

aperture mask: color *picture tube* mask registering *RGB beams.*

APO—action print only: balanced print from *optical picture negative* (no sound track). Compare: *check print, dirty dupe.*

apple (full, half): rugged wooden box—or half box—used on *set* to raise apparent height of performers or *props.* Compare: *pancake, riser.*

appropriation: approved *estimated* cost of advertising campaign.

apron: stage edge protruding beyond proscenium arch.

ARB—American Research Bureau: audience market survey service, based on television viewing *diaries* distributed in October, February and May. See: *National ARBitron.* Compare: *Nielsen.*

arc: camera movement along a curved path. Compare: *truck.* Also: Brilliant electrical discharge resembling daylight *color temperature;* produced by passing *current* between two *carbon electrodes.* Used for illumination or theatrical film projection.

ARD: West Germany's nine-station "First TV Network." Compare: *ZDF.*

Armstrong: U.S. inventor (*FM,* superhetrodyne circuit).

A-roll: master *mixed video tape* sequence used repetitively during *video tape* editing to avoid re-*mixing.* Also: First half of any pair of *film* or *tape* elements for combination. Compare: *B-roll*.

Arri: (from *Ar*nold and *Ri*chter) ingenious lightweight "Arriflex" *reflex* motion picture camera, in *16mm* and *35mm* versions; initially designed for Wehrmacht.

ARRL—American Radio Relay League: *ham* organization (founded 1915).

art card: cardboard (usually black, 11" x 14" and *hot-pressed* in white) with type or designs for *film* or television camera photography. See: *title card*. Compare: *balop, telop*.

art department: personnel charged with design responsibility.

art director: design and graphics supervisor for an individual *production*. Compare: *designer*.

artists—artistes: in Britain, *players* and *extras* (the latter called *crowd*).

ASA: see *A(N)SI*.

ASC—American Society of Cinematographers: cameraperson's trade guild.

ASCAP—American Society of Composers, Authors and Publishers: trade guild protecting musical performance rights. Compare. *BMI, SESAC*.

ascertainment: *FCC licensing* procedure requiring *broadcast stations* to investigate local *programming* needs.

ASFP: Britain's Association of Specialized Film Producers.

ashcan: 1,000-*watt* (1*k*) *floodlight*.

ASI—Audience Studies, Inc.: television (in-theater) *audience* research organization.

aspect ratio: standardized relationship of film *frame* width to height, normally 4 to 3, or 1.33:1; *widescreen* is usually 2:1; Cinemascope is 2.66:1.

assemble: *edit*-on additional material. Compare: *insert*.

assembler: in Britain, *editing* rank between *assistant editor* and *editor*.

assembly: selected *daily footage,* spliced into correct *scene* order. Compare: *rough cut*.

assignment—allocation: *FCC license* of specific *frequency* and *power* to a *broadcast station*. See: *call letters*.

assistant cameraman: general assistant to *cameraman* or *director of cinematography,* checking camera and *focus,* changing *lenses* and *magazines,* etc. Called *focus puller* in Britain.

assistant (or associate) director—AD: indispensable "detail man" on set or location—before, during and after *production.* Called *production secretary* in Britain. Compare: *gopher.*

assistant editor—editorial assistant: chore-handling assistant to *editor.*

associate producer: general assistant to *producer.*

A.T.&T.—American Telephone & Telegraph Company: communications conglomerate (active in early *radio broadcasting*).

atmosphere: in Britain, background sound *level;* ambient noise.

ATR: *audio tape recorder.* Compare: *VCR, VTR.*

ATS—automatic transmission system: self-monitoring, self-adjusting *transmitting* equipment requiring little or no engineering supervision.

ATS-6—Applications Technology Satellite-6: powerful all-purpose *NASA* communications *satellite,* launched in 1974 with 30-foot *antenna* to utilize higher *transmission frequencies.*

attenuate: decrease *signal level.*

attenuation loss: *signal* loss in cable, *attenuator, coupling* or other device when passing electrical *signal;* usually expressed in *decibels.*

attenuator: device decreasing *signal amplitude.* See: *fader, pot, volume control.*

ATV—Associated Television: one of British *IBA's "Big Five"* (the *Central Companies*).

A2: see *SFP.*

audience: (for research) group of *viewers/households* able to hear/view a *broadcast.* See: *broadcast home.*

audience accumulation: research survey count of gross audience buildup through repeated *exposures.* See: *frequency.*

audience composition: obsolete research survey classification, replaced by *demographic* statistics.

audience flow: half-hour research survey count of television *viewers* who (1) remain tuned to same *channel,* (2) switch to another, (3) turn their *receiver* on or off.

audience net unduplicated: research survey count—once—of *broadcast homes,* even when they receive subsequent *transmissions* of the same *program* series or *commercial.* Compare: *duplication.*

audience potential—sets-in-use: obsolete research survey count of home *receivers* actually switched on during a specific time period. See: *HUR, HUT.*

audience share: research survey percentage of total (local or national) *households* with one or more television receivers switched on during a specific time period. See: *rating.* Compare: *share.*

audience total: research survey count of all *HUR's* (or *HUT's*) tuned to same *program* for at least five minutes.

Audimeter: one of 1,200 electronic *Nielsen* audience *rating* devices measuring *receiver* usage in television "sample" homes. See: *SIA.*

audio: (from Latin "I hear") *recorded* or *broadcast* sound. Compare: *video.* Also: *Storyboard* or *script* "words." Also: Loosely, the sound recordist.

audio frequency: normally audible sound wave (between 15 and 20,000 *Hz*). Standard *audio frequency* ranges are *bass* (0–60 *Hz*), *mid-bass* (60–240 *Hz*), *mid-range* (240–1,000 *Hz*), *mid-treble* (1,000–3,500 *Hz*), *treble* (3,500–10,000 *Hz*).

audio mix: electronic combination of two or more sound elements into single final *track,* usually against *synchronous* picture projection.

audion: electronic *amplifier tube* invented by *DeForest,* 1906.

audio tape: non-*sprocketed* plastic tape in various widths, coated with magnetizable metallic oxides to *record* or *re-record* sound. Available (on cores) up to 7,200 feet. Compare: *video tape.*

audition: test *talent* prior to selection and hiring. See: *first refusal.* Compare: *book, hold.*

Auntie: *IBA* epithet for the *BBC.*

Auricon: *blimped 16mm single system camera.*

auto balance: automatic red/blue *color balance* detection/compensation system.

autochroma: automatic *equalization* of *VTR* color *saturation*.

autocue: in Britain, device rolling up a large *script* in performer's view. When mounted above camera, performer reads (by way of a 45° half-silvered mirror)—while looking directly into *lens*.

auto light range: automatic operating range of television *camera* at specified *output*.

automatic brightness control: *servo* control of *brightness* as function of *ambient* light.

automatic frequency control: *servo* control of oscillator *frequency*.

automatic gain circuit: *vidicon* camera *circuitry* adjusting *target* voltage to *ambient light* conditions. Compare: *AGC*.

automatic iris: camera *lens* device compensating for changes in *brightness levels*.

auto-parallax: system of interchangeable cams matching *viewfinder* angle to different *lenses* of non-*reflex* camera.

availability—avails: *broadcast* time open for purchase. Also: *Talent* available for specific *booking*.

available light: existing *location* light source.

average audience: research survey count of *broadcast homes* tuned to an average minute of the same program.

azimuth: perpendicular relationship of *magnetic head gap* to tape travel direction (should be exactly 90°).

B

baby: 400-*watt spotlight*.

baby legs: low camera *tripod*.

baby pup: in Britain, 500-*watt spotlight*.

back: add musical accompaniment.

backdrop: see *drop*.

back focus: distance from *focal plane* to rear of a *lens* set at *infinity*. Also: Focus a *zoom lens* at *"in"* position.

background—BG: *setting* behind performers. Also: Continuing music or sound source played at low *level*. Also: Atmospheric *signal* noise.

background projector: optical device generating graphic images on *rear projection* screen; usually for live television. See: *vizmo*.

backing: in Britain, *set* area seen through doors and windows. Also: See *base*.

backing copy: in Britain, first *video tape duplicate* off air *master*, for *protection*.

backlight: illumination striking subject from behind (or back-and-side), increasing background separation. See: *rimlight, triangle*. Compare: *key, fill light*.

back lot: major *studio* area used for *exterior* shooting.

backpack: portable (back-carried) television *recording* or *camera signal transmitting* equipment. Compare: *portapak*.

back porch: 4.77-*microsecond* portion of composite *video signal* lying between the trailing edge of *NTSC horizontal sync pulse* and the trailing edge of corresponding *blanking pulse.* (Does not include *color burst.*) See: *breezeway.* Compare: *front porch.*

back (screen) projection—BP: in Britain, projection of *still* or *motion picture* as scenic *background.* Normally used for scenes where background is relatively small—e.g., looking through a car or room window. Compare: *reflex projection.*

backspacing: *VTR editing* technique to insure proper equipment speed at moment of *signal transfer.*

backstage: area behind performance area *backgrounds,* etc.

backtime: synchronize program material backwards.

back-to-back: consecutive pieces of broadcast material.

backup: *standby* protection.

baffle: acoustical adjustment panel. See: *gobo.*

Baird: British television pioneer.

bait-and-switch: low-priced-item advertising "come-on."

balance: adjustable relationship between two or more elements. Also: Evenly *print film scenes* of varying color, *density,* etc.

balance stripe: extra strip on *magnetic-striped* film (opposite main *stripe*) to provide flat winding.

balloon: television *signal* distribution technique, utilizing balloons tethered between 10,000 and 15,000 feet, covering ten times the area of a normal *broadcast antenna.* Compare: *antenna, satellite.*

balop(ticon): *B*ausch & *L*omb television *camera chain* device transmitting small (4″ x 5″) opaque *art cards.* See: *telop.*

banana plug: testing *connector.*

band: sequential location of material on phonograph *disk.* Also: Specific area of *broadcast transmission frequencies.*

banding: *video tape playback head* speed distortion, characterized by evenly distributed horizontal variations in color *hue.* See: *velocity compensator.*

bandpass: *circuit* elimination of undesirable *frequencies.*

bandshaping: reduction of *Q* and *I signal bandwidths* to fit allotted color *transmission.*

bandwidth: number of *rf-modulated signal frequencies* contained in a designated *channel*. Telephone bandwidth capacity is 3,000 *Hz; AM* radio, 10,000 *Hz; high-fidelity audio tape,* 20,000 *Hz; FM* radio, 200 *KHz;* U.S. television, 6 *MHz; coaxial cable, 57 MHz;* optical fibers, multi *GHz.* See: *sideband.*

bank: equipment or lighting instrument group. See: *strip.*

BAPSA—Broadcast Advertising Producers Society of America: advertising *agency commercial producers'* group.

BAR—Broadcast Advertisers' Report: advertising research service monitoring (network or market) *commercial* use.

bar: musical *score* division.

bar line: in Britain, horizontal line area moving upward in television picture of ordinary *film screen* projection; and vice versa.

barn doors—flippers: adjustable metal side and/or top shades to narrow *luminaire beam.*

barn door wipe: optical imitation of opening doors.

barney: weatherproof protective film camera cover, usually sound-absorbent. Compare: *blimp.*

barracuda: telescopic *luminaire* support braced between floor and ceiling.

barrel: television image *sweep* distortion. Also: *Lens* system tube. Also: **barrel—bin:** *editing* receptacle with cloth bag holding un*spliced* lengths of sorted *film* hung from *pin rack.*

barrel marks: *lens* indicia.

bars: see *bar test pattern, color bars.*

bar sheet: see *lead sheet.*

barter—trade out: originally, station practice of selling fringe air *time,* usually through third party, for non-monetary considerations. Currently, a form of free *program syndication* with several syndicator commercials emplaced. Compare: *due bill.*

bar test pattern: color—b/w—*Q* and *I signal* check.

base: roll *film* substrate coated by light-sensitive *emulsion;* formerly cellulose nitrate, since 1952 nonflammable acetate, in thicknesses ranging from 0.0003″ to 0.0009″. Also: Plastic *audio* or *video tape* substrate coated with magnetizable metallic oxides; common *tape* bases are polyester and mylar (replacing acetate). Also: *Makeup* foundation.

base light: general light source. See: *ambient light, fill light.* Also: 225 (approx.) *candelas* required for television *studio* camera operation.

BASF: major German electronics manufacturer.

basher: in U.S., 500-*watt* circular *floodlight.* In Britain, *camera light.*

basic network: minimum group of scattered *affiliates* offered by a *network* for national advertising commitment. Compare: *regional.*

bass: standard *audio frequency* range (0–60 *Hz*). Compare: *midbass, midrange, mid-treble, treble.*

bassy: see *boomy.*

bat blacks—bat down: evenly adjust television *picture* black tones.

bath: *laboratory film developing* tank.

batten: horizontally suspended pipe for hanging *luminaires* or scenery.

battery: device storing *DC* electric power. See: *lead acid accumulator, nickel-cadmium.*

battery belt: rechargeable power cells worn by *hand-held* camera operator. See: *power pack.*

battery light: small portable *luminaire* with self-contained power supply.

bay—dock: *studio* storage area for scenic *set* pieces. See: *flat.* Also: **bay:** equipment mounting *racks.*

bayonet: spring-loaded camera *lens* twist mount (unthreaded).

bazooka: overhead *luminaire* support.

BBC—"Beeb"—British Broadcasting Corporation: government corporation established in 1922 to control Britain's noncommercial *broadcasting.* See: *Auntie.* Compare: *FCC, ORTF, RAI.*

BBDO—Batten, Barton, Durstine & Osborn: major advertising *agency.*

BBTV—British Bureau of Television Advertising: television advertising trade development organization. Compare: *TVB.*

BCU—big close-up: in Britain, performer's features. Also called (*LCU*) *large close-up* or *big head*.

beam: unidirectional pinhead electron stream generated by *cathode gun*. Also: Directed light flow from focusable *luminaire*.

beam angle: angle containing 50% of *spotlight* output.

beam lumens: amount of light within *beam angle*.

beam projector—parabolic—sun spot: *spotlight* projecting narrow, almost parallel light *beam*.

beam splitter: *lens* prism system: 1. separating reflected image light into *RGB* components; 2. diverting small amount of reflected image light into camera *viewfinder*. See: *mirror shutter*.

bear trap—gaffer grip—gator grip: heavy-duty *set* spring clamp, often with *luminaire* mount.

Beaulieu: compact French 8/16mm camera.

beauty shot: product *close-up*. Called *pack shot* in Britain.

beep(s): brief *1,000-Hz tone* signal(s) used for *audio cueing*. Compare: *punch*.

beeper: tone generator placing recurrent audible *signal* on phone line advising speaker he is being recorded.

bel—B: see *decibel*.

Bell & Howell Filmo: *16mm* television news camera.

bells—"on bells": audible warning (usually followed by continuously flashing red signal lights) before sound is recorded on *set*. Also: **bells:** wire *service bulletin* signal.

below the line: "technical"—as distinguished from "creative"— *program* costs. Compare: *above the line*.

belt pod: single-leg camera-to-waist-pouch support.

benchwork: see *animation camera*.

bending: television picture *distortion* caused by improper *video tape/playback head* timing coordination. See: *flagging, hooking*.

best boy: *set* electrician's assistant.

Betamax: *SONY* "home" *video tape recorder/playback* unit with special *cassette*.

BCN: Bosch Fernseh 1″ *video tape* configuration utilizing 190° *omega wrap*.

BFI—British Film Institute: association of cinema buffs. Compare: *AFI*.

BG—background: *setting* behind performers. Also: Continuing music or sound source played at low *level*. Also: Atmospheric *signal* noise.

bias: reference electrical *level*. Also: High-frequency *AC* carrier *current* (50–100 *kHz*) combined with *audio signal* in a magnetic *recording circuit*, to minimize nonlinear *distortion*.

bias light: "wiping" feature of lead oxide television camera *pickup tube*, reducing *lag* or *blooming*.

bicycling: physical exchange of *film prints* and *video tapes* between non-connected *stations* for staggered *programming*. See: *DB*. Compare: *network feed*.

bidirectional: (microphone) *response* in two back-to-back directions.

bifilar: *AC transfer video tape duplication* using *master* and single *slave*. Compare: *dynamic duplication*.

big eye: 10,000-*watt floodlight*.

Big Five—Central Companies: *IBA's ATV, GRA, LWT, THS, YTV*.

big head: see *BCU*.

big screen: projected television *picture*. See: *Schlieren lens, Schmidt mirror*.

billboard: brief *sponsor* identification near beginning or end of *program*. Compare: *cowcatcher, hitchhike*.

billing: charge to *agency/client* for broadcast advertising *time* purchase. Also: Contractually-agreed *cast credits*.

billyboy: in Britain, heavy *dolly*.

bin—barrel: *editing* receptacle with cloth bag holding un*spliced* lengths of sorted *film* hung from *pin rack*.

binary: having only two states (on or off) or values (0 or 1) or charge (*positive* or *negative*).

binaural: two separate sound sources in a single *recording*, each intended for a different ear. Compare: *monaural*.

binder: material adhering magnetizable particles to *tape base*.

bin stick: in Britain, sorting *pin rack* above *editing bin* holding ends of sorted un*spliced film* lengths.

Bioscope: early *motion picture projector* (Skladanowsky Brothers, 1895).

bipack—DX: two *negative films* printed as one. Compare: *tripack.*

bird: *satellite.* Loosely, *transmit* by *satellite.*

bird's nest—buckle: *film* camera *jam.*

birthmark—address: *digital video tape retrieval* system, utilizing *cue track signals.*

bit: brief creative *business.* Also: Minor role. Also: Computer binary digit (0 or 1) transmitted at up to 6.3 million per second. Compare: *byte.*

bitchbox: small *low-fidelity loudspeaker* used during *audio recording* to check average home *receiver* response.

bit rate: speed at which *bits* are generated or transmitted.

BL: self-*blimped Arri* camera.

black: in Britain, call a labor boycott.

black body: theoretical substance both radiating and absorbing light with 100% efficiency. See: *color temperature.*

black box: any of several simulated-*broadcast* television audience research techniques. See: *non-air commercial.* Also: Any electronic device producing unusual or mysterious effect.

black burst: 3.58 *MHz subcarrier signal* maintaining *synchronization* during *fade* to black.

black level: darkest part of television picture, transmitted at minimum 30% *voltage* (0.3 *v*).

Black Maria: Edison's initial (revolving) *motion picture studio,* West Orange, N.J.

blackout: ban on live local airing of broadcast event (usually sports). Also: Sudden switch-off of all lighting. Also: In Britain, labor union boycott.

black reference: see *reference black.*

Black Rock: *Variety's* epithet for *CBS Inc.'s* New York corporate headquarters (located in Saarinen-designed black granite 51W52), matching *Thirty Rock* (*NBC*) and *Hard Rock* (*ABC*).

black velour: non-reflective *background drape.*

black week—dark week: one of four weeks a year in which *Nielsen* does not measure *network* television audiences.

blank(s): clear *animation cel(s)* used to maintain consistent photographic density. Also: Unrecorded *tape* or *disk*.

blanket area: *1 volt/meter* (1 V/M) *radio signal* reception area.

blanketing: broadcasting a *signal* in excess of 1 V/M, usually close to the *antenna*.

blanking interval: 10.5-*microsecond* interval during which television receiver *scanning beam* is suppressed by a blanking *pulse* while returning to left side of screen to *retrace* next *horizontal scan line*—or to top of picture tube (in 1.3 *milliseconds*) to begin another *field* (the latter move called *vertical interval* in Britain). See: *front porch*.

blanking level: level separating *synchronization* from *picture* information in *composite* television *signal*.

blanking pulse: see *blanking interval*.

blast filter: see *pop filter*.

blasting: performing with excessive *audio level*.

bleachers: moveable *studio* audience seats.

bleed: framing out part of television picture. See: *crop*.

bleep—blip—bloop: brief *1,000-cycle tone* signal for *soundtrack cueing*. Also: *Synchronizing tone* at 2-second (3-foot) visual *cue* on *film leader*. Also: *Erase* unwanted *soundtrack* words.

blimp: soundproofed *motion picture camera housing,* eliminating motor noise. Compare: *barney*.

blinge: in Britain, distorted *optical dissolve*.

blip: reflected *CRT radar readout*. Also: See *bleep*.

block: work out camera and *cast* positions and movement in advance of *production*. Compare: *wing*. Also: Grooved device to *edit* and *splice audio tape*. Also: In Britain, low *set* platform.

blockbuster: (from World War II bomb) heavily promoted major *network program*.

block off—crush out: in Britain, create excessively illuminated surface causing undesirably white television picture area.

block programming: *network* strategy to influence viewer "carry-over."

blonde: *2K quartz-iodine lamp*.

bloom: undesirable television or film picture local halation, caused by excessive light saturation; eliminated in *solid-state* television cameras. Called *block off, crush out* in Britain. See: *bias light*.

bloop: see *bleep*.

blooper: amusing *live* error.

blow: stumble badly in performance.

blower brush: *camera/projector gate* cleaner.

blow up: enlarge optically, usually frame-by-frame from *16mm* to *35mm*. Also: Transcribe smaller formats to *2" quad video tape*. Also: **blowup:** *still* photograph enlargement.

Blue Book: (from its cover) 1946 *FCC* dictum on "Public Service Responsibility of Broadcast Licensees."

blue matteing: (earlier) *film* version of *chromakey video* technique. Compare: *rotoscoping, traveling matte*.

Blue Network: early *NBC* radio *hookup*, eventually becoming *ABC* Radio. Compare: *Red Network*.

blue pencil: edit (or censor) air material.

blurb: loosely, news *release*.

BMI—Broadcast Music, Inc.: trade association protecting musical performance rights. Compare: *ASCAP, SESAC*.

BNC: see *Mitchell*.

board: *control room console*.

board fade: diminishing sound *levels* from the *control room*. Compare: *live fade*.

board on end: in Britain, *clapper board* photographed (upside down) at end rather than start of *take*, for production expediency.

bodywash: dark *makeup*.

Bolex: spring-driven Swiss 8/16mm camera.

boob tube: denigratory reference to television *receiver*.

book: hire *talent*. See: *first refusal*. Compare: *audition*. Also: Hinged *flat*. Also: *Script* accompanying musical presentation.

boom: cantilevered camera *mount* of varying size and length. Called *jib* in Britain. Compare: *crane, dolly*. Also: Similar rod-like telescopic *mount* for suspended *microphone*.

boom down (up): reposition camera.

boomerang: *luminaire* holder for interchangeable color *gels*.

boom man: sound technician operating *microphone* boom. Called *boom swinger* or *boom operator* in Britain.

boom shot: high angle shot from cantilevered camera position.

boomy: marked resonance at lower end of *audio frequency* range, accentuating or prolonging low-pitched, "tubby" sounds. See: *bassy, lows.* Compare: *highs.*

bond: safety cord or chain securing suspended *luminaire.*

booster: equipment to amplify and retransmit a *signal.*

booth: small soundproof *studio* for isolated voice *recording* on *set* or *stage.* Also: *Clients'* observation room.

bootleg: illegally reproduced.

border—X-ray: overhead *luminaire* strip.

Bosch: major German electronics firm manufacturing *hand-held Fernseh* television camera. See: *ENG.*

bottle—bulb: glass envelope of television *picture tube.*

bounce: light source reflecting on subject. Compare: *key.* Also: Rapid changes in *contrast signal level* during television picture *switching.*

box: four-walled *set.* Also: Loosely, *audiotape cartridge.* Also: **box—gallery:** in Britain, *control room.*

brace: scenery support strut.

braceweight: slotted cast iron *brace* support.

BRC—Broadcast Rating Council: industry-established watchdog group to supervise audience research standards.

break: "time out" in *rehearsal* or *production.* Also: Move away from. Also: *Program* section set apart for *commercial announcements.*

breakaway: *prop* or *set* built to fall apart during violent on-camera action.

breakdown: analysis of *production* requirements.

breakers: in Britain, main control switches for *set* lights.

breakup: momentary television picture *distortion.*

breezeway: portion of *back porch* between trailing edge of *NTSC horizontal sync pulse* and start of *color burst.* Compare: *front porch.*

BRI—Brand Rating Index: annual national marketing survey covering brand consumption and preference.

bridge: connective *audio* link—sound or music—between two sections of a *broadcast*. Also: Connective picture continuity. Also: Two parallel connected *circuits*.

bridge—light bridge: walkway over *grid*. Called *gantry* in Britain.

brightness: see *luminance*. Also: *Pedestal* control on home television *receivers*.

brightness control: *rheostat* controlling intensity of *picture tube* electron *beam*.

brightness range: relative *luminance* values in a television picture. Compare: *contrast*.

bring up: raise *levels*.

British Actors Equity Association: theatre, film and television *artists'* union.

British Board of Film Censors: trade organization issuing certificates of audience acceptability.

broad: box-shaped 2,000-*watt floodlight* creating flat, even *set* illumination. See: *half broad*.

broadband: *bandwidths* above 3–4 *KHz*.

broadcast: see *broadcasting*.

broadcast band: standard *AM frequencies*.

Broadcast Bureau: *FCC* advisory division.

broadcast homes: household owning one or more radio or television broadcast *receivers*.

broadcasting: (from seed-sowing—originally U.S. Navy fleet instructions by wireless, c. 1912) *radio* or *television signal* transmission for public reception. Compare: *narrowcast, closed circuit*.

broadcast quality: equipment or *tape* designed or manufactured for over-the-air use. Compare: *air quality*.

B-roll: second half of any pair of *film* or *tape* elements for combination. Compare: *A-roll*.

brute: 10,000-*watt*, 225 *amp fresnel-lensed carbon arc spotlight*, used for poorly lit *locations*. Also called *10K*.

BSE: experimental Japanese *broadcast satellite*.

BSI: British Standards Institute. Compare: *A(N)SI, DIN*.

BTA—best time available: broadcast advertising scheduling left to station's discretion. See: *ROS*.

bubble: in Britain, incandescent light bulb. Also: (In Britain) overtime.

buckle—bird's nest: *film camera jam*.

budget: approved estimated breakdown of all *production* costs.

buff: polish *film* to remove scratches.

bug/eye—fish/eye: extreme *wide-angle lens,* mainly used for comic *close-up* effects. Compare: *telephoto*.

build up: in Britain, blank opaque film (black or white) spliced as spacing between sections of *workprint footage*.

bulb: glass or quartz envelope containing *lamp filament* or *fluorescent* material in gaseous element. Also: **bulb—bottle:** glass envelope of television *picture tube*.

bulk erase—mass erase: magnetic-field device to *degauss* all *recording tape* on a *reel* without unspooling. Compare: *erase head*.

bulletin: news development interrupting normal *broadcast programming*. Compare: *advisory*.

bull line: heavy-duty scenery rope.

bumper: extra *tail program* material. Compare: *cushion, pad*.

bump-in—bump-out: in Britain, instantaneously add or subtract new *optical* picture information to *frame*.

bump up: *dupe* in larger format.

burlap: coarse natural cloth material for *set drapery*. Called *hessian* in Britain.

burn—burn-in: retention of spurious image by television *pickup tube target* after change of subject. Called *burn-on* in Britain. (Removed by photographing a brightly lit white card.) Also: **burn in:** *superimpose* (a title).

burn-up: in Britain, area of clear *positive film* created by *negative overexposure*.

bus: common (usually uninsulated) central *circuit*. Also: Row of button controls on *video switching console*.

business: minor on-camera action. See: *bit*.

bust shot: performer framed waist-up.

busy: distractingly overelaborate.

butterfly: sunlight *diffuser* for *exterior filming*. Compare: *reflector*.

butt splice—butt weld: non-overlapping *film* join.

buy: approved performance of *scene*. See: *hold, selected take, print*.

buying service: media purchasing agent.

buyout: one-time *talent* payment for certain minor performance categories, not further compensated by re-use fees. Compare: *residual*.

buzz track: in Britain, recorded ambient noise used when spacing (opening up) *soundtracks*.

b/w—B & W: black and white.

B wind: see *A & B winds*.

B-Y: blue primary color difference *signal*.

byte: one-eighth *bit*.

C

CAB—Cooperative Analysis of Broadcasting: 1930's telephone audience research survey.

cable: electrical conductor(s) in protective sheath. Compare: *coax*.

cable guard: protective molding at base of television camera *dolly*.

cable ramps: flanking wedges protecting *cable* runs from *set* or *location* traffic.

cable TV: *transmission* (for a fee) of television *signals*—non-broadcast or "imported"—to home *receivers* (15% of all U.S. *television homes* in 1978) on a wired network whose *bandwidth* (162 *MHz*) can theoretically accommodate 50 *channels*. Initiated 1950 in Lansford, Pa. See: *CATV, distant signal*.

calibration: *focus* and *aperture* check of mounted *lens*.

calibrations: indication on *animation* art background showing amount of movement between *frame* exposures.

call—call sheet—call board: production timetable for *talent* appearance.

call letters: assigned *broadcast station* identification. In U.S. (with a few historic exceptions), "W"-prefixed, east of Mississippi River; "K"-prefixed, west. See: *allocation*.

cameo: foreground lighting against dark background.

camera—cam.: optical or electronic instrument for recording images.

camera card: large card for television photography, carrying program *titles* or *credits*. Compare: *crawl, cue card*.

camera chain—chain: a *camera*, its *cables, video* controls, *monitor* and power supply.

camera chart: in Britain, animator's *layout* sheet.

camera cue: in Britain, red light atop television camera indicating when its shot is being transmitted.

camera light: camera-mounted light for close performer illumination. Called *basher* in Britain. See: *eye light*. Compare: *tally light*.

cameraman: chief camera technician determining visual components of a shot. Called *lighting cameraman* in Britain.

camera original: exposed *film* from a camera.

camera rehearsal: dress rehearsal to *block* camera movement and *switching*.

camera report: camera operator's *take-by-take* record, with instructions to film *laboratory*. Called *camera sheet, dope sheet, report sheet* in Britain.

camera right, camera left: movement directions (from camera's point of view). Compare: *stage right, stage left*.

camera tape: see *gaffer tape*.

camera test: brief *negative* end section exposed for initial *laboratory* development testing. Compare: *cinex, wedge*.

camera trap: niche concealing camera in scenery.

camera tube: *pickup tube* converting optical images into electrical *signals* by electronic *scanning* process. See: *iconoscope, image isocon, image orthicon, Plumbicon, SEC, SIT, vidicon*. Compare: *picture tube*.

cam head: see *gear head*.

campaign: varied advertising for specific product over specific period of time. Compare: *schedule*.

can: metal container for *film* transportation or storage ("in the can" = completed). Also: 1,000-*watt floodlight* (*ashcan*).

candela (cd): 1936 replacement for the *foot candle* (= 1.02 candelas) as *luminance* standard.

cans: *headphones*.

canned: *pre-recorded*. See: *HFR*.

canoe: in Britain, section of curved *quad* video tape between *VTR* guides.

Canon 35: 1937 Bar Association dictum denying photographic access to courtroom proceedings (extended to cover television, 1963).

canting: tilting camera for "crooked" shot. See: *dutch.*

CAP: Britain's Code of Advertising Practice. Compare: *NAB Code.*

cap: *lens* cover.

capacitance: storage of electric energy in an electric field, measured in *farads.* Compare: *inductance.*

capacitor: *capacitance* device replacing obsolete *condenser.*

capstan: motorized rotating *spindle* to *transport recording tape* at fixed speeds. Compare: *pinch roller.*

capstan servo: *helical VTR head phase* and *tape speed* control system insuring proper sequential reading of *video* information.

caption: superimposed *subtitle,* usually translated dialogue. Compare: *title.*

caption roller: in Britain, roll-up *program credits.*

caption scanner: in Britain, small *b/w* television camera for *superimposing* artwork, *titles,* etc.

capture ratio: ability of *FM receiver* to discriminate between two *signals* at the same *frequency.*

cap up: cover television camera *lens.*

carbon: obsolete, simple variable-*resistance microphone,* 400 to 4,000 *Hz* capability.

carbons: *DC arc* light (or its *electrodes*).

cardioid: *microphone* with heart-shaped *pickup* sensitivity area.

card rate—rate card: *broadcast station*'s standard advertising charges, broken down by time of day, length of message and frequency of insertion.

carnet—tempex: European customs form covering temporary equipment importation.

carpark: in Britain, *program filmed/taped* in studio's parking lot.

carrier: *frequency wave transmitting radio* or *television signals.*

CARS: community *antenna* relay station.

cart—cartridge: container holding single *tape* or *film feed reel* that must be *threaded* to *take-up reel* in playback/projection system (or run as endless loop). Compare: *cassette, reel-to-reel*. See: *video cartridge, video cassette*. Also: **cartridge:** *phonograph pickup* device *transducing stylus-groove* patterns into electrical impulses.

cassette: container holding pair of *reels*—one to *feed* (and *rewind*), the other to *take up tape* or *film*. See: *video cartridge, video cassette*. Compare: *cartridge, reel-to-reel*.

cast: to select *talent*. See: *audition, book*. Also: Descriptive list of *program talent*. See: *billing, credits*.

cast commercial: *broadcast* advertising message utilizing *program talent*.

casting director: individual handling *talent audition* and selection.

catadioptric: *lens* with mirrors in optical path to shorten *barrel*.

cathode: *negatively* charged *terminal*.

cathode ray tube—CRT: device containing electron *gun emitting* continuous controlled *beam* of electrons against internal charged or *phosphorescent screen*. See: *hard copy, soft copy, yoke*.

cattle call: indiscriminate mass *talent audition*.

CATV—community antenna television: subscriber television reception serving an entire geographic area through *cable* connections from a single *master antenna*. Compare: *CCTV, MATV*.

catwalk: latticed walkway over *grid*.

CB—citizen band: 40-channel *short wave broadcast band* in the 27 *MHz* range for private communication (8–10 miles, subject to *sunspot interference*).

CBC—Canadian Broadcasting Corporation: state-controlled radio/television *network* (annual tax support = $25,000,000). Compare: *CRTC*.

CBS—CBS Inc. (formerly **Columbia Broadcasting System):** U.S. conglomerate *broadcasting network*. See: *Black Rock*.

CCD—charge-coupled device: solid state sensor. *Image CCD:* postage stamp-sized grid with more than 160,000 light-sensitive diodes—replaces *vidicon* tube in miniaturized *television cameras*.

CCIR—Comité Consultatif International de la Radiodiffusion: international *transmission* standard-setting organization (established 1927).

C clamp: spring-loaded clamping device (usually incorporating a *luminaire* mount). In Britain, also called *G clamp*.

CCR: see *central control room*.

CCTV—closed-circuit television: non-*broadcast transmission* of any television *signal* to a *receiver*. Compare: *CATV*.

CDL: computerized *video tape editing* system.

Ceefax: (''see facts'') British *(BBC)* system for *digital transmission* of printed information, utilizing *television signal blanking intervals* at seven *megabits* per second. See: *ORACLE*. Compare: *ANTIOPE, SLICE, Teletext, Viewdata*.

cel: (from ''cellulose'') transparent plastic sheet, usually 11″ x 14″ with *''pegged''* alignment holes, on which *animation* artwork is sequentially inked or painted (U.S. technique, developed by Hurd, 1906). See: *blank(s), animation board*.

cel flash: *hot spot* caused by uneven *cel* surface.

cellular system: optimized 900 *MHz* computer-controlled urban relay network (1½ mile spacing) ''handing off'' mobile radio telephone *transmissions*.

cement: solvent used to pressure-join a *film splice*.

centisecond: 1/100 second.

Central Companies: *IBA*'s *''Big Five'': ATV, GRA, LWT, THS, YTV*.

central control room—CCR: in Britain, *broadcast* facility control center.

centre: in Britain, plastic hub (unflanged) for reeling or storing film.

century stand: one-piece, three-legged telescoping metal pipe support, with each leg at different height to permit close stand grouping. Compare: *spud, turtle*.

ceramic: low-quality *microphone;* proper sound reproduction fails around 8,000 *Hz*. Compare: *condenser, crystal*.

CH—critical hours: period in which broadcast *signals* can cause interference. See: *daytimer, PSA*. Compare: *clear channel, powerhouse*.

chain—camera chain: a *camera,* its *cables, video* controls, *monitor* and power supply.

changing bag: simple cloth bag *"darkroom"* with armholes for location *film magazine* loading in daylight without *fogging* risk.

channel: *FCC*-assigned broadcast frequency: for television, 6 *MHz* wide; for *FM,* 200 *kHz* wide. Also: Complete sound or *signal circuit.*

character generator: electronic *matteing* device for "instant" television picture *titling.* See: *edging.* Compare: *code generator.*

charge-coupled device: see *CCD.*

charge hand: in Britain, union foreman.

charger: electrical device restoring power to discharged *batteries.*

charts: trade-paper lists of best-selling records.

chaser: sequentially wired row of lamps giving effect of light "movement." Also: Music accompanying performer's exit.

chassis: electronic equipment frame or mounting.

cheat: "non-realistic" camera position, used to improve picture composition.

checkerboarding: *film editing* technique utilizing *A & B rolls.* Also: Every other day (or week) *program* scheduling.

check print: quick non-*balanced print* from newly completed *optical picture negative* to check mechanical *printing* errors. Often used for *dubbing.* Called *slash print* in Britain. Compare: *APO, dirty dupe.*

cherry picker: motorized high-angle camera position inside operator bucket. Compare: *crane, parallels.*

chest shot: performer framed waist-up.

chief engineer: "in-charge" *control room* technician. Called *transmission controller* in Britain.

china girl: identical *negative leader frame*(s) of an American girl's face, used as color standard by U.S. *film laboratories.* Compare: *lily.*

china marker: wax-base film marking pencil. Called *chinagraph* in Britain.

chinese: combination *pull back* and *pan.* Also: Horizontal *barn-door* position.

chip: filament thrown up by cutting *stylus.* Called *swarf* in Britain. Compare: *fluff.* Also: Base for *semi-conductor integrated circuit;* about ⅛" square, contains many *transistors.* See: *microprocessor.*

chip chart—chips: standard *b/w* test-swatch chart for television camera *alignment.* Compare: *grid.*

chippy: in Britain, *set* carpenter.

choke: inductive device impeding *current* flow.

chroma—intensity: measure of color *hue* and *saturation* (undiluted with white, black or gray.)

chroma control: television *receiver* control regulating *saturation.*

chroma detector: *b/w circuitry* eliminating *color burst* by sensing absence of *chrominance signal.*

chromakey: television (mainly video tape) *matteing* technique, usually with a vast difference in size relationships; the subject matted is placed against a background (usually blue) and the signal is mixed with that particular color channel suppressed. Also called *inlay.* Called *color separation overlay* (CSO) in Britain. Compare: *blue matteing, process shot, rotoscoping.*

chromatic: pertaining to color television.

chromatic aberration: color *wavelength* dispersion within a defective *lens,* creating different focal points as color fringe haloes.

chromaticity: see *chroma.*

chrominance: color camera *channels* for television's red, green and blue (*RGB*) *signals.* Also: *Colorimetric* difference between a color and *reference white* of the same *luminance.*

chromium dioxide—CrO₂: non-compatible *audio tape* coating offering improved *signal-to-noise ratio.* Compare: *cobalt-energized.*

churn: *cable subscriber* turnover.

CHUT—cable households using TV: audience survey estimate of unduplicated *households viewing* television during average quarter-hour time period.

CIA—Central Intelligence Agency: U.S. government unit secretly funding *Radio Free Europe* and *Radio Liberty* since the 1950's ($60,000,000 annually).

CID: charge-injection device.

cinching: improperly tight and damaging *film* or *tape* winding.

cinch marks: random vertical black stripes in a *film print*, caused by overtight *negative* winding. Called *stress marks* in Britain.

ciné board: *16mm footage* of actual *storyboard frames*, edited against a *soundtrack*.

Cineorama: 1896 ten-projector 360° *motion picture* presentation.

CinemaScope: *wide-screen film* process; 2.35:1.

cinematographer: supervisor of *motion picture camera* operation.

cinéma vérité—direct cinema: *documentary film* style imposed upon non-*documentary filming*. See: *slice*.

Cinerama: *wide-screen film* process: 2.59:1.

cinex—synex: fifteen-*frame laboratory* test strips of key *film scenes*, each *frame* printed with slightly different *balances* for final *release print* color selections. Called *pilots, clip roll, four-framer* in Britain. Compare: *camera test, wedge*.

Circarama: 360° screen film process.

circle of confusion: size of *lens*-formed image point.

circuit: interconnected electrical system. Also: Chain of *motion picture film* theaters.

circular polarization: improved—right-handed corkscrew (circular)—television *signal transmission* pattern; reflective *ghosting* is minimized by left-handed polarity shift. Compare: *horizontal polarization*.

circulation: net unduplicated count of *television homes* or individuals actually *viewing* a *network* or single *station* during a week or month.

CISAC—Conference International de Societé des Auteurs et Compositeurs: trade association of musical performing rights organizations.

clambake: badly produced program.

clamping: establishing a fixed reference DC *video level* at beginning of each *scanning line*.

clamping disk—knuckle: adjustable *century stand* head, grooved to accept pipe *booms, flag* stems, etc.

clapper boy—clapper loader: in Britain, the camera assistant handling the *slate* (or *clapper board*). See: *board on end.*

clapstick—clapboard: special hinged *slate* device for picture-and-sound *synchronization,* inscribed with full production information and "clapped" on camera before each *double-system take.* Called *clapper board* or *number board* in Britain.

class A,B,C,D: broadcast advertising time periods, graded by audience size. Also: **Class A,B,C:** *FCC* 3 *kw* to 100 *kw station* classification.

Class I,II,III,IV: *FCC*-assigned *AM frequencies* with 250*W* to 50 *kW* operating power.

class rate: dollar cost breakdown of *broadcast time* costs.

claw: camera/projector mechanism pulling each successive *frame* down into the film *gate* while the *shutter* is momentarily closed. Compare: *pins.*

clean entrance (exit): camera operation before *action* begins (and after it ends) for *editing* purposes.

clear: arrange necessary permissions for use. Also: Arrange *transmission* of *network program* with *affiliate(s)*. Also: **clear (filter):** protective *lens* covering.

clear channel: (usually *AM*) *radio station* dominance (10 *kW* to 50 *kW* operating power) over a wide geographic area, free from competitive *transmission interference.* Compare: *CH, daytimer, PSA.*

clear the frame: call to clear area in front of camera during rehearsal.

Clerk Maxwell: Scots physicist postulating existence of *radio waves* (1867).

click track: *synchronized* music recording beat track, fed only to conductor's *headphones.*

client: agency or advertiser buying broadcast time. See: *account, sponsor.*

Clio: gold statuette awarded annually to outstanding *commercial* work by judges of *American Television & Radio Commercials Festival.* Compare: *Emmy.*

clip: short section of longer *film* or *tape*. Also: Shear off *signal peaks*. Also: Accidentally omit a note, syllable or word from beginning or end of *audio track*.

clipper: *switcher clipping* control knob.

clipping: removal of *signal* portion above or below pre-set level. Also: Illicit *station* practice of substituting *local* for *network commercial* for double payment.

clip roll—four-framer—pilots: in Britain, laboratory film test strips of *color balance* ranges prepared to determine final *printing light* selections.

clogging: *tape oxide* buildup on *recording* or *playback head,* causing improper *tracking* or *tape* damage.

closed circuit—CCTV: non-*broadcast transmission* of any television *signal* to a receiver. Compare: *CATV*.

closed set: private *filming* or *taping* activity.

close-up: see *CU*.

cloud wheel: *set* device projecting sky effect on *cyc*.

cluster bar: multiple *luminaire mount.*

clutter: excessive transmission of non-*program* materials (*commercials, promos,* etc.), often up to 25 per cent of *prime broadcast time.*

C-mount: 1″ diameter *16mm lens mount.*

CMX: magnetic *disk* storage system for conveniently *editing* video tape.

coax—coaxial cable: "hollow" ¾″ television *signal transmission cable* carrying 20–40 *channels,* offering low power *loss* at high *frequencies,* with *repeater amplification* every ⅓ mile. First installed 1935 between New York and Philadelphia. Compare: *fiber optics, microwave, satellite, triaxial.*

cobalt-energized: compatible *audio tape* coating offering improved *signal-to-noise ratio*. Compare: *chromium dioxide.*

code: union *talent* agreement.

code generator: equipment recording visual identification signals onto *video tape*. Compare: *character generator.*

coercivity: amount of magnetic energy, measured in *ø̸ersteds* (after discoverer of electromagnetism) required to affect normal *video tape* particle patterns.

cogwheel effect: *microsecond* displacement of alternate *scan lines;* creates staggered vertical image.

coherer: early wireless wave detector (Branly, 1891).

Cohu tube: initial *ion-*accelerator device (1921).

coil: wire winding around *conductor* generating an electromagnetic field.

coincidental interview: telephone audience survey technique: "Are you viewing/listening?" (Poor at early/late hours; misses all homes without phones.)

cold: without preparation. Also: Bluish or greenish picture tone. See: *cool.*

color: atmosphere or mood.

color balance: proper adjustment of color elements to give subjectively satisfying *film* or television picture; usually based on skin tones.

color balanced: *film emulsion* allowing pure light of specified *color temperature* to appear as white in final *print.* Compare: *unbalanced.*

color bars—SMPTE standard test bars: electronically generated bar-shaped *video tape leader test pattern* to match *playback* to original *recording levels* and *phasing.* Usually accompanied by *1,000-Hz audio* reference *tone.* See: *bar test pattern.*

color burst: 3.58 *MHz subcarrier* frequency primary color relationship sample at *back porch* of each *scan line,* timed to a quarter-millionth second, *synchronizing transmitted* color *signals* to a *receiver.* See: *chroma detector.*

color compensating filter: *lens* filter effecting overall *color balance.*

color correction: readjustment of individual color components to match camera/lighting requirements.

color encoder: equipment reconstituting *NTSC* color *signal* from separate *RGB inputs.*

color film analyzer: electro-optical device scanning a color *negative* to establish proper *printing exposures.* See: *Hazeltine.* Compare: *china girl, lily.*

color frame: *luminaire gel-*support.

·43·

colorimetry: technical characteristics of any electronic color reproduction apparatus.

colorizer: device arbitrarily mixing television *color signals* with *luminance signals* for non-realistic color effects.

color killer: see *chroma detector*.

color media: any *transparent* material (glass, *gel,* etc.) placed in front of light source to alter color.

color response: *output* of *b/w* television camera relative to color subject.

color separation overlay—CSO: in Britain, television *matteing* technique.

color separations—separation positives: individual *b/w film* records of each of the three color components of a *negative,* for protection and *opticalling.* See: *prism block, Technicolor, Vidtronics.*

color shift: visibly annoying *transmitted* color change.

color subcarrier: see *subcarrier*.

color television: *transmission* of three separated (*primary color*) *signals,* superimposed at the *receiver* for illusion of full color.

color temperature: measurement (in *degrees Kelvin* [°K], 273.16° lower than centigrade scale) of relative color of a light source; the temperature to which a *black body* must be raised from absolute zero to radiate light of a specific color (higher temperature = bluer light; lower temperature = pinker light). Unrelated to *brightness*.

color wheel: early (*CBS*) television *transmission* technique.

COLTRAM—Committee on Local Television and Radio Audience Measurement: research methodology group.

combination rate: tie-in rate reduction for advertising over two or more *broadcast stations*.

combined: in Britain, "married" *film print* containing both picture and *soundtrack*.

comet tail: bright television *picture tube* smear created by moving *hot spot* or light source. Eliminated by *solid-state* cameras. Compare: *lag*.

coming up: the *program* following.

commentary over—out-of-vision—OOV: in Britain, performer heard but not seen.

commentator: news analyst. Also: In Britain, neutral *on-* or *off-camera* performer telling *program* story.

commercial: paid *broadcast* advertising message, usually *10, 20, 30* or *60* seconds long. See: *clutter.* Compare: *counter commercial.*

commercial broadcasting: *programming* "underwritten" by *sponsored* advertising.

commercial program: *broadcast* containing paid advertising.

commercial protection—product protection: *broadcast station's* formal minimum time interval between competing *commercial* messages. See: *separation.*

common carrier: organization required to lease its transmission facilities to all applicants. *Broadcast stations* exempt under Federal Communications Act of 1934 (see *FCC*).

comopt: in Britain, *composite film print* with *optical* (rather than *magnetic*) *soundtrack.*

Compact: *Philips*-licensed standard audio *cassette.* Compare: *EL-CASET, Unisette.*

compandor: device compressing/expanding voice *modulation.*

compatibility: ability of *b/w* television set to receive *transmitted* color *signals* with minimum picture *distortion.* Compare: *non-compatability.*

compere: in Britain, show host.

component: equipment item.

composite: "married" *film print* containing both picture and *soundtrack.* Called *combined* in Britain. Compare: *interlock.* Also: Combined *video signal, vertical* and horizontal *blanking* and *synchronizing signals* in a television *transmission.* Compare: *non-composite.* Also: Different photographs of same *talent* on single print. Compare: *head sheet.*

composite master: original completed *video tape.*

compression: *audio recording* technique minimizing excessive *level* variations to prevent *distortion.* Also: Reduction in television *signal gain* at one particular *level.*

Comsat—Communications Satellite Corporation: private "public" firm, serving as U.S. *Intelsat* member as well as establishing and maintaining *Intelsat's* various international *geosynchronous satellites. Comsat's earth stations* are operated by *A.T.&T.* Compare: *Domsat.*

Comsat General: operating subsidiary of *Comsat.*

Comstar: *Comsat General's satellites* used by *A.T.&T.* and General Telephone.

condenser: *spotlight* focusing *lens.* Also: High-quality *microphone* (invented in 1916). Compare: *ceramic, crystal.* Also: Obsolete *capacitance* device, replaced by *capacitor.*

conductor: medium transmitting electric *current.* Compare: *dialectric.*

cone: huge reflective *floodlight*—750 to 5,000 *watts*—illuminating large *set* areas.

Conelrad: (from *con*trol of *el*ectromagnetic *rad*iation) discontinued government-engineered *broadcasting* control system (in event of nuclear attack?). See: *EBS.*

confirmation: *station* acceptance of *broadcast* advertising order.

conform: match *off-line VTR edits* to 2" *quad video tape* (analogous to *film negative matching*).

conkout: equipment failure.

connector: *circuit* linkage. See: *female, male.*

console: *control room switching* desk.

contact print: *positive* film printed from *negative* in direct physical contact with identical width *raw stock.* Compare: *reduction print.*

CONTAM—Committee on Nationwide Television Audience Measurement: *network* watchdog group formed in 1963 to police audience *rating* practices.

contamination: incomplete separation of color *signal* paths.

contemporary: "top 40" popular music *radio station format.*

continuity: prepared *script* material. Also: Smooth flow of dramatic events in proper order.

continuity girl: in Britain, clerk recording all *set* action.

continuity sheets: in Britain, detailed production records kept by *continuity girl.*

continuous printer: film *laboratory* machine printing *optical track negatives.* Compare: *step printer.*

contract: *talent* or union agreement.

contractor: musical talent group supervisor. Also: In Britain, commercial *broadcast* group supplying *IBA programming.*

contrast: see *hard.*

contrast—contrast ratio: highest *luminance* value of television picture divided by lowest. See: *video gain.* Compare: *saturation, brightness range.*

contrast range: camera ability to distinguish between shades of gray (television, 30 to 1; film, 100 to 1). See: *gray scale.*

contrasty: lacking middle tones, thus of poor reproductive quality.

control ring: device raising/lowering television camera *pedestal.*

control room: small room for *production* management, usually higher than performing *studio* and separated from it by soundproof window and "sound lock." Called *gallery, box* in Britain.

control track: section of *video tape signal* controlling *playback synchronization.* Also used for *retrieval* coding.

convergence: electronically focussed three-color *beam* crossover at *aperture mask.*

convergence pattern: television test *signal* checking *monitor* picture for camera *scanning linearity, aspect ratio* and geometric *distortion.*

convergent lens: bi-convex, planoconvex or convergent-miniscus *lens;* forming real (positive) images. Compare: *divergent lens.*

conversation: "phone-in" *radio station format,* often deliberately insulting. Compare: *talk show.*

conversion filter: *lens* attachment re-*balancing film* (*emulsion*) for different light conditions. See: *daylight filter.*

converter: equipment translating television *signal* characteristics—number of *lines,* number of *fields* and color coding—from one national standard to another for international *transmission.* Also: Auxiliary device enabling *television receiver* to accept additional *channel* transmissions.

cookie—cucaloris—cuke: cut-out screen in front of light source, casting random-patterned wall shadows. Called *gobo* or *ulcer* in Britain.

cool: slightly bluish or greenish television picture. Compare: *warm*.

co-op: *broadcast* advertising cost shared by manufacturer and local distributor.

copy: advertising words.

copy platform: basic creative word (or picture) plan to exploit reputed product differences.

cording: visual identification—with string, tape or plastic tabs—of portions of *film footage*. Called *papering* in Britain.

core: plastic hub (unflanged) for *reeling* or storing *film*. Called *centre* in Britain.

Corgi and Bess: putative *BBC* epithet for Queen's annual Christmas *broadcast*.

coring out: eliminating *signal noise* by *digital* conversion.

corporate campaign: advertising directed at selling a firm's "image," as distinct from its products.

corrected (print): see *release print*.

corrective commercial: *FTC*-ordered *broadcast* advertising message prepared by advertiser to correct original misleading information. Compare: *counter commercial*.

costumes: performers' *wardrobe*. Also called *frocks* in Britain.

costume house: *wardrobe* rental agency.

countdown: one-second indications (from 10 to 2) on *video tape* or *film leader*, to permit exact *cueing*.

counter: *tape recorder* digital "footage" indicator.

counter commercial: unpaid *broadcast* advertising message— usually prepared by public interest group—countering misleading *commercial* information. Compare: *corrective commercial*.

counter-key—modelling: illumination source opposite *key light*.

counter-programming: *broadcast* planning to exploit competitive schedule weaknesses. Compare: *roadblocking*.

country and western: *radio station* musical *format*.

coupler: device to join lengths of *cable* possessing same electrical characteristics. Also: Telephone-to-*audio recorder* connection.

cove—ground row: *cyc* baseboard (usually concealing *luminaire strip*).

coverage: geographic area, usually designated in terms of the counties normally reached by any *level* of a *broadcast* signal. Also: Audience survey measurement of *receivers* in use.

coverage map: idealized contouring of *broadcast station's signal* reception strength. See: *blanket area*.

cover shot—insurance: wide camera position, *protection* for *jump cut lip sync close-ups*. Compare: *cutaway*.

cowcatcher: *sponsorship* announcement preceding *program's* actual start. Compare: *hitchhike, billboard*.

CP: *broadcast station* Construction Permit, issued by *FCC*.

CPB—Corporation for Public Broadcasting: government-funded group established under Public Broadcasting Act of 1967 to enhance non-*commercial* television *programming*. See: *PBS, NET, ETV*.

CPM—cost-per-thousand: index of *broadcast* advertising viewing audience effectiveness, expressed in dollars.

cps—cycles-per-second: obsolete unit of *frequency*. See: *hertz*.

crab: *dolly* sideways. Also: In Britain, metal floor brace for camera *tripod*.

crab dolly: hand-propelled camera + operator mount on which all wheels can be swivelled synchronously for sideways movement. Compare: *spyder*.

cradle head: camera *mount tilting* up or down on cradle-shaped rockers. See: *gear head*.

CRAM—Cumulative Radio Audience Method: 1966 *NBC* investigation of audience survey methodology.

crane: oversized camera + crew *boom*, usually mounted on truck. "To *crane*" = move *boom* up (down). Compare: *dolly*.

crank: operate a *motion picture camera* (from days of non-motorized cameras).

crawl: *drum* or scroll-mounted "roll-up" *program credits*, often *superimposed* over a picture. Called *creep, roll, caption roller* in Britain. Compare: *camera card, draw cards, flip cards (stand)*.

credits: opening or closing list of *program* personnel. See: *billing*.

Compare: *main title*. Also: Music performance point counts to establish composer *royalties*.

creep: *video tape/capstan* slippage, affecting picture *playback synchronization*. Also: In Britain, roll-up program *credits*.

creeper: performer edging too close to *microphone* or camera. Also: Low camera *dolly*.

creepie-peepie: *hand-held* television camera.

crew: loosely, *production* workers other than performing *talent*.

CRI—color reversal intermediate: *single-strand 16mm printing negative* optically compiled from sections of *original camera negative*. Also: **CRI—color rendition index:** numerical evaluation of effects of light source on visual appearance of surface.

crib card: in Britain, *live* television cameraman's *shot list*.

crispening: *digital* picture information recirculation, for a sharper image.

critical frequency: *frequency* below which (subject to seasonal variations, etc.) *radio signals* are reflected from—instead of passing through—the *ionosphere*.

crop: exclude edges of camera picture by tighter *framing*. See: *bleed*.

cross: performer's move across *set,* usually at right angles to camera.

crosscut: in Britain, rapid picture-to-picture alternation.

cross-fade: allow one *audio* source to rise from another.

cross-plug: *broadcast* advertising mention of *alternate sponsor*.

crosstalk: extraneous electronic leakage or *signal interference*. Also: *Video* color "bleeding."

crossing the line: changing camera position by more than 180°, resulting in viewer confusion *re:* subject action.

crossover network: *circuit* dividing up *signal* into its different *frequencies*.

cross-own: control television *station* and newspaper in same market. Compare: *duopoly*.

crowd: in Britain, supplementary *on-camera* performers.

crowd noise: low-level background conversation effect. See: *omnies, walla-walla*.

crowfoot: metal floor brace for film camera *tripod*. Called *crab* or *spider* in Britain.

CRT: see *cathode ray tube*.

CRTC—Canadian Radio and Television Commission: government agency regulating both *CBC* and private *broadcasting* re: *programming* requirements, etc. Compare: *BBC, FCC*.

crush: electronic intensification of television *picture black/white levels*.

crush out—block off: in Britain, excessively illuminate a surface, creating undesirably white television picture area.

crystal: low-quality *microphone;* proper sound reproduction fails around 8,000 *Hz*. Compare: *ceramic, condenser*.

crystal sync: wireless system *synchronizing* camera with *audio recorder*.

CS—close shot: in Britain, performers waist-up. Also: **CS:** Japanese *satellite* program.

CTAGB—Cable Television Association of Great Britain: British *cable* system operators' membership organization.

CTS—Communications Technology Satellite: joint U.S.-Canadian *Hermes* equatorial *satellite,* launched 1976; 40 times more powerful than *Intelsat* series, utilizes solar energy.

CTW—Children's Television Workshop: public television *production* company.

CU—close-up: performer's head and shoulders. Called *big close-up (BCU)* or *large close-up (LCU)* in Britain. Compare: *MCU, ECU*.

cue—Q: sight or sound signal to commence (or cease) *action*.

cue card: *off-camera* prompting card in performer's view. See: *idiot card*. Compare: *camera card, prompter*.

cue mark: projectionist's changeover warning, usually several *frames* of a tiny white circle in advance of *film's* beginning or end. Called *cue dot* in Britain.

cue sheet: written collection of sequential *cues,* usually for *audio mixing*. Called *dubbing chart* in Britain. Also: *Optical* cameraman's or *animator's* layout sheet. Called *camera chart* in Britain.

cue track: auxiliary *audio recording* area on *video tape*.

cumulative audience—cume—reach: number of unduplicated broadcast *program* (or *commercial*) *viewers* over specific number of weeks.

Curie point: temperature at which magnetic *tape* loses its residual *recorded signal*.

current: electron movement through *conductor;* rate measured in *amperes*.

cursor: moving dot on *character generator* screen indicating letter entry position.

cushion: expandable or contractable *program* section. Compare: *bumper, pad*.

cut: call to halt *action*. Also: Instantaneous picture change. Compare: *dissolve*. Also: *Edit* film. Also: Eliminate material. Also: Separated section on a phonograph *disk*. Also: Groove an *acetate phonograph recording* with a *stylus*.

cutaway: *film* or *video tape* shot of interviewer (or other material of secondary importance); avoids *cover shot* or *jump-cut* editing of interviewee. Called *nod shot* in Britain.

cutback: edit return to a previous *scene*.

cut-in: *local station broadcast* material (often an alternate *commercial*) inserted in *network feed*. Compare: *tag*.

cut key: in Britain, *intercom* on/off switch.

cutoff: section of *transmitted* television picture information hidden by home *receiver mask*. See: *Academy aperture, reticule*. Compare: *safety*. Also: In Britain, *high* or *low frequencies* (or both) eliminated from *audio signal*.

cutter: *film editor*. Also: Thin opaque shape to screen *set luminaire*. See: *finger, flag*. Compare: *dot, gobo, mask*.

cutting copy: in Britain, *editor's* rough combination of picture and *soundtrack*.

cutting ratio: in Britain, relationship of *exposed film stock* to final *edited footage;* average around 7 to 1.

cutting room: *film editor's* workshop.

cutting sync—edit sync: *frame-for-frame synchronization* of *work picture* and *soundtrack* with no allowance for *film pullup*. Called *level sync* in Britain. Compare: *printing sync*.

cyan: greenish-blue subtractive element of color *negative film;* the complementary of (and producing) red. See: *magenta, yellow.*

cyc—cyclorama: large J-profiled piece of *background scenery,* usually white, eliminating any visual frame of reference. See: *limbo, no-seam.* Compare: *set, milk sweep.*

cycle: repeated photographed *animation* drawing movement. Also: Arbitrary period of *broadcast commercial* use—usually 8 or 13 weeks.

D

DA: *directional antenna.*

DAC—digital-to-analog converter: equipment regenerating *digitally* transmitted *signals* to original *analog* form. Compare: *ADC*.

dailies—rushes: film *positives* processed overnight from previous day's original *negative* photography. See: *one-light.*

dark: unused facility.

dark current: *photoconductor* current flow in total darkness.

darkroom: lightproof area for *film* loading, unloading and processing. See: *changing bag, fog, safelight.*

dark week—black week: one of four weeks in the year in which *Nielsen* does not measure *network* television audiences.

DATE: *PBS digital* television system *transmitting* four additional *high-fidelity audio signals.*

dawn patrol: early-morning *broadcasters.*

day-for-night: underexposure (with *neutral density filter*) approximating nighttime effect with film shot in daylight. (Avoids labor penalty for night work.)

daylight filter: *lens conversion filter* permitting use of daylight-*balanced film emulsions* under artificial light conditions.

day part—time: *broadcasting* period for *commercial* advertising sale. See: *daytime, drive time, fringe evening time, prime time.*

daytime—housewife time: broadcast *time* sale classification: 10:00 A.M. to 4:00 P.M. See: *time.*

daytimer: radio station licensed for daylight-only operation (*signal* improvement after dark creates *coverage interference*). See: *CH, PSA.* Compare: *clear channel, powerhouse.*

DB—delayed broadcast: local *station transmission* of previously *broadcast network program* by means of *film* or *video tape recording.* See: *bicycling.* Compare: *network feed.*

db meter: control device indicating *audio levels.* See: *decibel.*

DBS: direct *broadcast satellite.*

DC—direct current: electronic power supply flowing constantly in a single direction (polarity). Compare: *AC.*

dead: inoperative or failed equipment. Also: Without *acoustical reverberation.* Also: Discarded creative material. Compare: *live.*

dead air: *broadcast transmission* without picture and/or *audio signal.*

deadline: last date for receipt of material for *broadcast.*

dead side: low-response side of *microphone.* See: *pickup.*

deaf aid: performer's (usually newsperson's) inconspicuous *cueing earphone.*

dealer spot: *open-end commercial* with added local retail outlet identification. See: *tag.* Compare: *cut-in.*

dealer tie-in: *network commercial* message listing local retail outlets.

debug: correct technical malfunction.

decamired: 100,000, divided by any °K (*Kelvin*) value—for a more workable *color temperature* rating. See: *mired.*

decay rate: fade-out rate of electronic *signal* or picture.

decibel—db: (after inventor of the telephone) unit of *loudness* measured on a logarithmic scale. The human ear can detect 1 db changes in *loudness,* from 0 to 130 decibels.

decisecond: $^1/_{10}$ second.

deck: stripped *audio tape transport* system (with *heads* but no *amplifier* or speakers). Also: Portable *VTR.* Also: *Studio floor* level.

decoder: color television *receiver circuitry* between *signal* detector

and *picture tube*. Also: Device un*scrambling cable* television *feed*.

definition: perceivable detail of visual reproduction.

deflection coil: *cathode ray tube yoke* winding, controlling *scanning beam*.

defocus: deliberate camera image "softening," usually as transitional effect. Compare: *dissolve*.

DeForest: inventor of *audion* (electronic *amplifier tube*), 1906.

degauss: (after propounder of mathematical theory of electricity)
erase previously *recorded tape* in a magnetic field, by realigning all particles in a regular pattern. See: *bulk erase*.
Also: Remove stray magnetism from any (metallic) *recording, editing* or *playback* equipment.

degaussing pencil: electromagnetic tool for delicate *soundtrack
editing*.

degrees Kelvin—°K: measurement of light source *color temperature*. 0 °K is − 273.16° C; each °K = 1° C.

demagnetizer: electromagnetic tool for *degaussing tape recorder
heads*.

demodulate: extract *broadcast signal* from *carrier wave*.

demographics—profile: breakdown of *broadcast* audiences by
varying statistical characteristics, such as sex, age, family
size, education and economic level. See: *audience composition*. Compare: *psychographics*.

dense: *overexposed negative*. Compare: *thin*.

designer: *set* technician supervising scenic and *property* construction and installation. Compare: *art director*.

densitometer: *film density* measurement device. Compare: *sensitometer*.

density: degree of opacity; light transmission *vs*. reflectance.

depth of field: distance range (increasing with smaller *lens aper-
tures*) through which scene elements remain sharp. Compare: *depth of focus*.

depth of focus: distance between *lens* and *film* in which sharp *focus*
is maintained. Compare: *depth of field*.

deuce: 2,000-*watt floodlight*.

develop: process a *latent* image on *exposed film*.

DFS—Dancer-Fitzgerald-Sample: major advertising *agency*.

DGA—Directors Guild of America: *film* and television *directors'* professional group.

dialectric: non-*conductive* material.

diascope: illuminated television camera *alignment lens* attachment.

dialogue: performed conversation.

diaphragm—iris: adjustable *aperture* of overlapping metal leaves controlling amount of light passing through *lens*. See: *stop*. Also: *Microphone* soundwave sensing element.

diary: self-reporting audience survey technique, often automated.

DICE—digital intercontinental conversion equipment: British (*IBA*) bi-directional international television picture *field*-rate *digital* converter, making 6,000,000 calculations per second (world's fastest computation).

dichroic: selective light *filter* (transmitting certain *wavelengths*, reflecting others) often used to convert *tungsten* or *quartz* light source to daylight *color balance*. See: *macbeth*.

dichroic mirror: television camera color *filter* selectively separating red, green and blue (*RGB*) light components for their appropriate *camera pick-up tubes*. Compare: *stripe filter*.

dielectric: *insulating* material.

differential gain: *amplitude* change of color *subcarrier* as function of *luminance*.

differential phase: *phase modulation* of color *signal* by *luminance signal*.

diffuser: material used to spread or soften illumination. Called *jolly* in Britain.

digital: translation of information into mathematical *bits*, providing easy *signal* regeneration without *noise, drift* or *distortion*. Compare: *analog*. See: *ADC, DAC*.

digital counter: *tape recorder* "footage" indicator.

dilute: reduce color saturation by adding white.

dimmer: device controlling illumination *brightness*.

DIN: Deutsche Industrie Norm *film emulsion speed rating*. Compare: *AS(N)I, BSI*.

diode: *vacuum tube* ("oscillation valve") invented by Fleming in 1904, based on electronic phenomenon observed by Edison

21 years earlier. Contains *negative filament* (*cathode*) and *positive plate* elements. Can be used as a *rectifer*. Compare: *pentode, tetrode, triode.*

diopter lens: supplemental screw-on optical element to shorten *focal length* for *close-up* photography. Compare: *long lens, telephoto.*

diplexer: equipment permitting *transmission* of television sound and picture signals from same *antenna.*

dipole: *FM antenna.*

dipstick: in Britain, *AGB* audience research survey.

direct cinema—cinéma vérité: *documentary* film style imposed on non-documentary filming. See: *slice.*

directional: *microphone* with narrow ''lane'' of *pickup sensitivity.* Compare: *non-directional.* Also: Phase-controlled (*antenna*) radiation.

director: in-charge person on *set* or in *studio.*

director of cinematography: *film production* title or rank above *''cameraman.''*

direct positive—reversal: *camera-original film* producing a *positive* image when developed, eliminating intermediate *negative* and *printing* steps.

dirty dupe: *one-light single-strand* duplication of *work picture.*

direct response: *commercial* urging immediate purchase by mail or telephone.

discount: see *frequency discount.*

discover: reveal something by a camera move.

discrete: *quadruphonic audio broadcast* or *recording/playback* system, utilizing four *audio signals* on one *FM channel* or four-channel *tapes* or *disks.* Compare: *matrix.*

discrete component: individual *circuit* device.

dish—dishpan: large concave *antenna.*

disk: *grooved audio recording.* Also: *Video tape slow-motion* or *freeze frame* equipment (introduced in 1965). See: *slow-mo.* Also: New technique for inexpensive mass production of television recordings—utilizing *laser* beams, metal *styli,* etc.

disk jockey: *radio* record show host.

disk pack: grouped *video disks* storing *recorded* information.

disk recorder: *video recorder* utilizing a single magnetizable *disk* (*slow-mo*) or *disk pack* to store information. Compare: *video disk*.

display: visual *readout*.

dissector: early (*Farnsworth*) experimental television *camera pickup tube*.

dissolve (lap): fading into new *scene* while fading out of old. Compare: *cut, defocus*.

distant signal—imported signal: *cable* television *programming* taken off the air outside system's normal reception area and forwarded for local distribution.

distortion: electronic departure from desired *signal*. See: *harmonic distortion, intermodulation distortion*.

distribute: route an electric *signal* (or *current*).

distribution amplifier: electronic device feeding television *signal* at original *level* to several *monitors* without *loss*.

divergent lens: bi-concave, planoconcave or divergent-miniscus *lens,* forming virtual (negative) images. Compare: *convergent lens*.

dlt.: daylight.

DMA—designated market area: *Nielsen audience* survey research market classification, denoting the county cluster in which most *viewers* watch the local *station*. Compare: ADI.

Dobson: in Britain, final *rehearsal* before a complicated performance.

dock—bay: *studio* storage area for scenic *set* pieces.

documentary: recorded presentation of actual, unrehearsed events. Compare: *cinéma vérité, direct cinema, slice*.

dog: unsuccessful creative work.

Dolby: (after inventor): patented *audio bandpass circuitry* improving *signal-to-noise ratio* by manipulating *high-frequency* response.

dolly: wheeled camera + operator mount of varying complexity. Compare: *crane*. Also: *"In"* or *"out"* move of such mounted camera (altering *parallax*).

dominant area: see *ADI*.

Domsat: *dom*estic (U.S.) communication *sat*ellite system.

dope sheet: in Britain, *camera operator's take-by-take* record, with instructions to *film laboratory*. Also called *camera sheet, report sheet*.

dot—target: metal disk used as *flag*.

double: play more than one part. Also: Star's impersonator for distant and/or difficult shots.

double broad: box-shaped 4,000-*watt fill light*.

double clad: *scenic flat* with designs on both sides.

double 8: *16mm reversal film* with twice the normal number of *sprocket holes* along both edges; split after (*8mm*) *exposure* and *development* into two *8mm* strands.

double head: in Britain, projection of separate but *synchronized work picture* and *magnetic soundtrack*.

double headset: *intercom* with separate *circuit* for each *earphone*.

double perf(oration): *16mm* silent *film stock* with *sprocket holes* along both edges. Compare: *single perf*.

double print: *printing* each *frame* twice to halve apparent speed of an *action*. Called *double frame* in Britain. Compare: *skip frame*.

double re-entry: complex television *switcher* controlling complicated *optical effects*.

double sprocket: see *double perf*.

double system: simultaneous picture and sound *recorded* separately in different media (i.e., on *film* and *audio tape*) for later *synchronization*. Compare: *single system*.

double take: identical *film action* from different angles *edited* (overlapped) incorrectly.

doughnut: wraparound recorded *commercial* material (usually music) enclosing *live copy*.

down converter: equipment altering *satellite microwave frequency* to *VHF* television *signal*.

downgrade: reduce *commercial talent* status; i.e., from *player* to *extra*. Compare: *outgrade*.

downlight: directly-overhead *luminaire beam*.

downlink: *satellite*-to-ground *transmission*. See: *earth station*.

downtime: period of equipment non-use.

downstage: stage area toward audience (or camera). Compare: *up-stage*.

downstream: see *down the line*.

down the line: towards *signal's* destination. Compare: *up the line*.

drain: *storage battery* power loss.

drape: unpainted hung fabric *background*. See: *velour*. Compare: *drop*.

draw cards: *art cards*—usually *titling* or *credits* stacked in a special holder—whipped out of frame horizontally in front of the television camera. Compare: *crawl, flip cards (stand)*.

dress: prepare a *set*. Also: Final *rehearsal* before *broadcast*. Compare: *dry run, run-through*.

dresser: wardrobing assistant.

drift: electronic *circuit's* inherent tendency to alter its characteristics with time and temperature changes.

drive pulses: television *blanking* and *sync pulses*.

drive time: *radio time* sale classification—A.M. (6:00 to 10:00) and P.M. (4:00 to 7:00)—when most commuting listeners are in automobiles. See: *time*.

drop: hanging painted canvas *background*. Compare: *flat, drape, profile*. Also: Measure of vertical height.

dropout: horizontal television picture *playback* streak, reflecting momentary lack of *video* information caused by *tape* (oxide) surface irregularities when *recording*. See below.

dropout compensator: complex electronic storage device to "fill in" *dropout* streak with previous line's picture information. See above.

drop shadow: *title* lettering with mechanically or electronically introduced screen "shadow" to improve legibility.

drudge: see *lexicographer*.

drum: flywheel to insure smooth *film* movement past *projector sound head*. Also: Slotted *helical scan record/playback* head assembly. Also: Rotating *slide* holder. Also: Rotating *title/credit* mount.

dry: in Britain, completely forget one's lines.

dry cell: waterless storage *battery*. See: *flashlight battery, nickel-cadmium*. Compare: *wet cell*.

dry run: *rehearsal* without *costumes,* camera *facilities,* etc. Compare: *run-through, dress.* Called *stagger through* in Britain.

dual track: see *half track.*

dub—dubbing: electromagnetic *duplication* of *audio* or *video tape masters.* Also: Recording *lip-synchronized dialogue* against existing *film* picture (and often over existing *sound*) *loops.* (Called *looping* on West Coast.)

dubber: equipment for *recording* and *playing back magnetic sprocketed film.* Also: One *tape recorder* playing a *signal* into another.

dubbing chart: in Britain, written *cue* flow, usually for *audio mixing.*

dubbing theatre: in Britain, a *recording/mixing studio.* Also called *recording theatre.*

dub down: transfer 2″ *quad video tape* to smaller widths.

dub off: *re-record* portions of existing materials.

dub up: transfer smaller *video tape* widths to 2″ *quad.*

duct: protective *cable* pipe.

due bill: *station's* exchange of *broadcast time* for advertiser's actual product or services. Compare: *barter.*

dulling spray: wax-base aerosol spray to reduce reflective surface shine.

dump: drop a *feed.* Also: Destroy. See: *junk.*

duopoly: ownership of two or more *broadcast* facilities in a single market. Compare: *cross-own.*

dupe (duplicate): copy of *film* or *tape recording* (the latter also called *dub*). Compare: *master.*

dupe neg: *b/w duplicate* made by *finegrain* from original *negative material.*

duplex(er): single *conductor* (or equipment) accepting/*transmitting* two different *signals* (or *feeds*). Compare: *multiplex, simplex.*

duplication: see *dupe.* Also: Cumulative research total of *broadcast homes* or individuals exposed more than once to the same *transmitted* material. Compare: *audience net unduplicated.*

dutch: angle a camera position. See: *canting.*

dutchman: canvas strip covering hinge between two *flats*. Also: Condensing *lens* for *plano-convex spotlight*.

DVE: *digital video effect* generator.

DX—bi-pack: two *negative films* printed as one. Compare: *tripack*. Also: **DX:** *short wave* contact between distant *transmitters*.

dye transfer: *printing* stage of *Technicolor film* process.

Dynalens: vibration-damping liquid *lens* mount.

dynamic: pressure-sensitive *microphone* whose *diaphragm* is connected to moving coil in magnetic field.

dynamic duplication: *AC transfer* system using *video tape master* and several *slaves*. Compare: *bifilar*.

dynamic range: softest-to-loudest sound range reproducible by any piece of equipment without *distortion*.

E

Early Bird (later **Intelsat I**): initial 85-pound commercial *geo-synchronous satellite,* capable of 240 telephone *circuits* or one television *channel;* launched April 6, 1965, operational through 1968.

earphone—earpiece: tiny wired speaker worn in the ear. Compare: *headphones.*

earth: in Britain, zero *voltage* point in an electrical system.

earth station: ground facility for receiving *satellite transmissions.*

EBR—electron beam recording: high-quality *video tape-to-film transfer* system, utilizing *step printing* of 3 *b/w negatives.*

EBS—Emergency Broadcast System: government-engineered (nuclear attack?) warning system electronically commandeering all U.S. *broadcast stations.* Replaced *Conelrad* in 1960's. Also used in peacetime disasters.

EBU—European Broadcasting Union: multi-national *programming* organization.

echo: duplicate (leading or lagging) of primary *signal.*

Echo A: initial (but defective) reflective orbital *satellite* balloon, launched by *NASA* May 13, 1960. See: *Echo I.*

echo chamber: acoustic or electronic device adding about 2 seconds *reverberation* to an *audio signal.*

Echo I: successful 100 ft. diameter reflective orbital *satellite* balloon, capable of a single transcontinental telephone call, launched by *NASA* August 12, 1960. Followed by **Echo II** (135 ft. diameter). See: *Echo A, Telstar.*

Eclair: *16/35mm* French interchangeable-*magazine* camera.

ECU—extra close-up—extreme close-up: performer's features. Called *BCU* (*big close-up*) in Britain. Compare: *CU*.

edge-fogged: in Britain, *film footage* ruined by inadvertent *exposure* to light.

edge number: multi-digit identification number applied by *film* manufacturers to each foot of *negative raw stock;* numbers print through onto *positive work print footage* (for *reprinting* and *negative matching* during film completion). Note: A new and different set of *positive* edge numbers can always be ink printed. Called *key number* in Britain. Compare: *time code.*

edge stripe: *magnetic audio recording stripe* laid onto *edited* positive *film print* (or part of *original reversal raw stock*).

edging: *character generator's* electronically-produced letter shadows.

edit: creatively alter original *recorded* order (and/or length) of *film* or *tape* material.

edit code—time code: *SMPTE* standard *video tape retrieval* system (similar to *motion picture edge number* identification), usually recording an eight-digit *address* (hours, minutes, seconds, *frames*) on *control track*. Compare: *talking clock.*

editing machines: two basic types—"vertical," *film* passing down from *feed reel;* "horizontal," *film* passing left to right from *feed plate*—all with various trade names.

editing ratio—ratio: relationship of *exposed film stock* to final *edited footage;* average around 7 to 1. Called *cutting ratio* in Britain.

edit(ing) sync(hronization)—cutting sync: *frame-for-frame synchronization* of *work picture* and *soundtrack,* with no allowance for *film pullup*. Called *level sync* in Britain. Compare: *printing sync.*

editor: *tape* or *film production house* specialist charged with piecing together a production from varied visual and sound elements.

editorial assistant—assistant editor: chore-handling assistant to *editor*.

educational (radio, television): see *non-commercial*.

E.E.: (*video tape*) electronic *editing*.

effects—EFX: visual designs generated electronically. Also: Extraneous sounds or *audio backgrounds*. Compare: *SFX*.

effects bank—effects switcher: *control room console* providing electronic *opticals*.

efficacy—lumens per watt: number of *lumens* produced by light source for each *watt* of power applied.

EFP—electronic field production: location use of portable *video taping* equipment.

EHF—extremely high frequency: *radio wavelengths* from 30-300 *GHz*.

EIAJ—Electronics Industry Association of Japan: standard-setting Japanese trade group.

eidophor: obsolete large-screen television projection equipment.

eightball: small round *non-directional microphone*.

8mm: obsolete *reversal film stock 8mm* wide. See: *Super 8*.

eight-track: *audio tape recorder/playback* handling eight separate *signals* on same *tape*.

EJ—electronic journalism: see *ENG*.

ELCASET: Japanese-licensed ¼″ audio cassette. See: *Unisette*. Compare: *Compact*.

electret: miniature charge-storing *circuit*. Also: Clip-on *microphone* incorporating same.

electrician: *set* lighting technician. Called *sparks* in Britain.

electrode: electric source *terminal*.

electrolysis: chemical change obtained by passing electric *current* through *electrolyte*.

electrolyte: *ionized* material (usually liquid or paste) conducting electric *current*.

electromagnet: soft iron core magnetized by electric *current* passed through surrounding *coil*.

electromagnetic radiation: radiant energy in form of invisible waves moving through space or matter.

electromagnetic spectrum: radiant energy range (low to high) of long, *low-frequency radio waves, microwaves,* infrared radiation, visible light, ultraviolet radiation. X-rays and gamma rays (all traveling at speed of light, 186,000 *mps*).

electron beam recording—EBR: high-quality *video-tape-to-film* direct *transfer* technique; utilizes *step printing* of three *b/w negatives.* Compare: *EVR.*

electron gun: *cathode-ray tube* device continuously emitting narrow focusable *beam* of electrons. See: *yoke.*

electronic bandspread: two-dial *short wave tuning.*

electronic editing: re-*recording* original *video tape signals* onto second *video tape* with changes in order and/or length without physical *splicing.*

electronic recording: conversion of *sound waves* into *recorded* electrical impulses. Replaced (1927) *acoustic disk recording.*

electrostatic: field produced by stationary electric charge. Compare: *magnetostatic.*

electrostatic (loud) speaker: device utilizing *capacitor* plate movement to *transduce* electric *signal* into *sound waves.*

elevation: drawing of vertical *set* surfaces.

ellipsoidal: *spotlight* with sharp, shutter-shaped *beam.*

ELF—extremely low frequency: *radio wavelengths* $< 300\,Hz.$

Emitron: early *BBC* television camera system.

Emmy: annual award for oustanding television *programming* by *American Academy of Television Arts and Sciences.* Compare: *Clio.*

EMP—Electromagnetic Pulse Project: U.S. Air Force missile-jamming program creating immense surges of radiant energy simulating lightning and nuclear explosions, capable of burning out power and communications *networks, broadcasting stations* and home television and radio *receivers.*

emulsion: light-sensitive coating placed on film *base; oxide* placed on *tape base.*

en banc: full *FCC* commissioner panel.

encoder: device altering character of an electronic *signal,* or *superimposing* other information on it. See: *color encoder.*

end rate: *broadcast station's* least expensive *commercial time* category. See: *class D.* Compare: *prime time.*

end slate: *slate* photographed (upside down) at end rather than at start of *take,* for *production* expediency. Called *board on end* in Britain.

ENG—electronic news gathering: television news *production* with *hand-held* cameras and *video casette recorders.* See: *Akai, Fernseh, Ikegami.*

engineering: *broadcast station's* technical group.

enhanced hand-held: gimballed, gyroscopically-balanced camera *mount* strapped to operator's body. See: *Steadicam.*

enhancer—image enhancer: television *signal* processor creating "crisper" picture.

EP: "extended play" 45 *rpm phonograph disk.*

EQ—frequency equalizer: control device to improve *audio* quality, usually by suppressing one of the five *frequency* ranges.

equalize: electronically compensate *frequency* and *level* characteristics of any *audio* or *video* source.

Equal Time: *Section 315* of 1934 Federal Communications Act guaranteeing similar *broadcast time* privileges to all candidates for same political office. See: *FCC.*

erase—degauss: *wipe* or neutralize previously *recorded* electromagnetic *signal* patterns prior to re-*recording.*

erase head: small *degaussing* device in *tape path,* removing previously *recorded signals* by realigning all magnetic particles into regular pattern. Compare: *record head, bulk erase.*

ERP: effective radiated power.

error rate: ratio of usage to malfunction.

ESS—Electronic Still Store: *CBS frame-store* device.

establishing shot: initial *master tape/film scene* identifying the location and/or relationship of *on-camera talent.*

estimate: assess economic cost of *production.*

ET—electrical transcription: archaic term for non-acoustic *disk* recording.

ethnic: *radio station format* featuring *programs* of specific interest to one or more minority groups.

ETS: Japanese *satellite* program.

ETU—Electrical Trades Union: British *set electricians'* labor union.

ETV—educational television: *non-commercial* scholastic television *broadcasting*. See: *NET*. Compare: *CPB, PBS*.

Eurovision: European television *program* distribution service.

ev—electron volt: *photon potential* difference; higher *ev* = higher *frequency*, shorter *wavelength*.

evaluate: determine surface quality of new *video tape raw stock*.

event: unit in a programmed sequence.

EVR—Electronic Video Recording: CBS-sponsored system for mass production of *video recordings* on special *film;* now abandoned (in the U.S.). Compare: *EBR*.

exciter lamp: *sound head* light source for *photoelectric cell* "reading" *film optical soundtrack*.

ex parte: unethical private contact (*i.e., broadcasters* and *FCC*).

Explorer I: initial U.S. orbital *satellite,* launched February 1, 1958. Compare: *Sputnik*.

explosion wipe: sudden *optical effect* bursting from center of *frame* outwards.

exposure: adjustment of light (radiant energy) falling on film *emulsion;* varied by controlling duration or intensity of light, or *camera lens aperture*. See: *overexpose, underexpose, rating*. Also: Number of times a *transmission* has been seen on television.

exposure meter—light meter: *photoelectric cell* device in various formats, measuring direct or reflected illumination *intensity* in *candelas*.

exposure rating: manufacturer's designated *film emulsion speed*.

exposure sheet: *cue sheet* for photographing *animation* sequence.

ext.—exterior: an outdoor *set* or *location*. See: *lot*. Compare: *int*.

extended play—45 rpm: popular single-*cut phonograph disk* rotation speed. Compare: *long-playing*.

extension tube—extender: device to hold *lens* away from camera for *close-up* photography. See: *diopter lens, proxar*.

external key: television camera *signal inlaying matted* image into *background*. See: *chromakey*. Compare: *plate*.

extra: supplementary *on-camera* performer. Called *crowd* in Britain. Compare: *player, stand-in*.

extreme close-up: see *ECU*.

extremes: important change-of-action drawings in an *animation* sequence (called *keys* in Britain). *In-between* material is handled somewhat mechanically.

eyeball: adjust visually.

eye light: low-level illumination (usually from camera-mounted lamp) producing *specular* reflection from performer's eyes and teeth.

eyeline: direction of performer's gaze.

F

f: mathematical symbol of relationship between *lens aperture* and *focal length*. See: *f-stop, stop*. Compare: *T-stop*.

FAA—Film Artists' Association: British extras' union.

faceplate: front of television *picture tube;* also its tri-color coated *phosphor* (dot or stripe) array.

facilities—fax: technical equipment—lights, cameras, *microphones,* etc.—for *rehearsing* or *broadcasting*.

facilities fee: in Britain, payment for use of *location*.

factor: exposure correction figure.

fact sheet—poop sheet: *copy* points for *announcer's ad-lib* use; opposite of prepared *script*.

fade: bring in (or out) slowly. Compare: *pop-on*.

fade-in: come slowly out of black picture to an image. Also: Come slowly out of silence to a sound.

fade-out: go slowly from an image to black. Also: Go slowly from sound to silence.

fader: sliding control console *rheostat* (slider) raising or lowering *audio* or *video levels*. See: *attenuate*. Compare: *pot*.

fader bars: manual levers for *switcher* transitions.

fading: *broadcast signal* variation, caused by time of day, weather, latitude, atmospheric or *sunspot interference*.

fairing: logarithmic speed attenuation (or increase) for smooth stop (or start).

fairness doctrine: *FCC* mandate that stations must offer *broadcast time* to "both sides" of public issues; upheld by U.S. Supreme Court, 1969.

Family Viewing Time: controversial "voluntary" restrictions by *networks* (heavily endorsed by FCC) on television violence-*programming* from 8:00 to 9:00 P.M. Judged illegal by lower courts, 1976.

farad: (after the 1832 electromagnetic pioneer) unit of *capacitance*.

farm: see *antenna farm*.

Farnsworth: U.S. television pioneer.

fast (slow): *emulsion* more (or less) sensitive to light. Fast emulsions tend to be grainy. Also: Indication of *lens* quality (fast—lower *f-stops*—transmits more light).

fast forward: high-speed transport of *tape* from *feed* to *take-up reel*, bypassing unneeded material.

favor: turn *microphone* or camera towards position of particular performer.

fax—facilities: technical equipment—lights, cameras, microphones, etc.—for *rehearsing* or *broadcasting*.

FCC—Federal Communications Commission: government agency set up under Federal Communications Act of 1934 to supervise all U.S. *broadcasting*. Compare: *Federal Radio Act, Radio Act*. Also compare: *BBC, CRTC, ORTF, RAI*.

Federal Radio Act—FRA: legislation passed by Congress in 1927, empowering a five-man Federal Radio Commission to issue three-year *broadcasting station licenses*. Replaced in 1934 by the Federal Communications Act. See: *FCC, Radio Act*.

feed: *transmit* a *signal* for *broadcast*.

feedback: *input* return of outgoing *signal* by design (such as striking multi-image effect obtained by pointing television camera at its own *monitor*); or default (such as high-pitched acoustic oscillation created by *microphone* picking up its own *speaker*, or by accidental closing of an *audio circuit*. Called *howl-round* in Britain.) Also: Electronic performance sampling for correction control.

feed plate: *editing table* horizontal *film* supply.

feed reel: *film editor/projector* or *tape recorder supply reel.* Compare: *take-up reel.*

feet: (non-metric) standard *film* length measurement; sixteen *35mm,* forty *16mm* and 72 *Super 8mm frames* per *film foot.*

female: *connector* receptacle. Compare: *male.*

femtosecond: one-quadrillionth second.

Fernseh: See: *Bosch.*

ferrite: metallic compound of high magnetic permeability, used for *video recording heads.*

Fessenden: U.S. radio pioneer (heterodyne *circuit*).

FET: field effect *transistor.*

fiberglass: reinforced plastic utilized for large lightweight *scenic props.*

fiber optics—OF—optical fibers: interference-free *laser beam* waveguide television system (postulated by Kao and Hockham, 1966) transmitting 167 *channels* on a single 90-*micron* flexible glass-fiber cable, with *repeater amplification* every 1.5 miles. See: *RTI.* Compare: *coaxial.*

fidelity: capability of *playback* system to fully reproduce original *signal.*

field: one-half a television picture *scanning* cycle, two *interlaced* (alternate *scan line*) fields to each *frame,* or sixty fields per second (fifty in Britain). Also: *Frame* area measurement, in horizontal and vertical steps of 10% each. Also: Depth of acceptable *lens* definition.

field angle: angle containing 90% of *spotlight's* output.

field frequency: number of *transmitted* television *fields* per second; 60 in U.S., 50 in Britain.

field of view: area seen through particular *lens,* expressed in degrees.

field sequential color: color information visually produced by successive *RGB fields.*

15 ips: professional *audio tape recording speed.* Compare: 7½ *ips.*

filament: *conductor* rendered *incandescent* (and emitting electrons) by passage of electric *current.*

fill: optional material if program runs short. Also: *Fill light.*

fill light: non-apparent light source supplying general illumination, reducing shadows or *contrast* created by *key* (subject) lighting. See: *ambient light, base light, triangle.* Compare: *backlight, rimlight.*

film: *sprocket-holed* rolls (usually cellulose acetate) of various widths, coated with light-sensitive *emulsion.*

film base: see *base.*

film chain: *film projector,* its related television camera, *cables, monitor, video* control and power supply. Also called *tele-ciné.*

film clip: short *film* section inserted in *live* television *program* or *commercial.*

film island: television *station's* group of *film* (and *slide*) *projectors.*

film loop: continuous *film clip* spliced *tail* to *head.*

Filmo: Bell & Howell *16mm* television news camera.

film plane: location of *film* in relation to *lens,* usually indicated by symbol on camera body. Compare: *focal plane.*

film speed: number of *frames* passing through *picture gate* each second. Also: Degree of *emulsion* light sensitivity.

filmstrip: *film* sequence of individual *35mm* or *16mm frames,* shown singly in special *projector,* with or without separate *synchronized soundtrack.* Compare: *slide film.*

film transfer: *filmed* copy of *live* or *video taped television tube* image. See: *EBR, kinescope, Image Transform, Vidtronics.*

film unit: *location crew.*

film videoplayer: (Kodak) device *projecting Super 8mm sound film* through standard television *receiver.*

filter: electric, electronic, optical or acoustical device rejecting *signals,* vibrations or radiations of certain *frequencies* while passing others.

filter factor: *exposure* multiplier to compensate for light reduction by a *lens filter.*

filter mike: *microphone* feeding a *circuit* with modified *frequency response (low frequencies* usually eliminated).

filter wheel: filter holder permanently fitted behind camera *lens.*

finder—viewfinder: special optical system or screen to show camera *lens framing.* See: *Academy aperture, reticule, safety.* Also: Adjustable device for that purpose worn around *cam-*

eraman's or *director's* neck. Also: Small television camera (*b/w*) component displaying camera's (or *line*) picture to cameraman.

fine cut: *editor's* final *work print*, ready for approval and *negative matching* with no further changes. Compare: *rough cut*.

finger: narrow opaque shape to screen *set luminaire*. See: *cutter, flag*. Compare: *dot, gobo, mask*.

finegrain: special *slow-speed film raw stock* with finer-grained *emulsion* and more transparent *base*, used for quality *duplication* of original *negative* material.

fire up: switch equipment on.

first generation: see *generation*.

first refusal: tentative *hold* on performer's services. Called *first call* in Britain. Compare: *book*.

fishbowl: *studio* observation booth, usually for *advertising agency* and *client* personnel.

fisheye—bugeye: extreme *wide angle lens*, mainly used for comic *close-up* effects. Compare: *telephoto*.

fishing rod—fishpole: long hand-held *microphone boom*.

five—5K: see *senior*.

525-line: standard number of horizontal *sweeps* per *frame* in Western Hemisphere (and Japan) television *transmission* systems (offering lower picture *resolution* than Britain and Europe's *625*).

fixed focus: *lens* holding subjects in *focus* at all distance settings.

fixed position: specified—rather than "open"—time period for *commercial*, sold at premium *rate*. Compare: *ROS*.

flag (French flag): on *set*, square shade (usually black cloth) attached to metal support in front of camera to shield *lens* from stray light. Also called *nigger* in overdeveloped countries. See: *cutter, dot, finger, gobo, mask*.

flagging: television *picture distortion* caused by incorrect *video tape-playback head* timing coordination. See: *bending, hooking, time base corrector*.

flagship: major *station* of a *broadcast network*.

flapover: in Britain, optical spin effect.

flapper—swinger: *flat* swung out of path of camera *dolly*.

flare: dark "burned-out" area on television *picture tube* caused by local light oversaturation (usually random reflections). Sometimes used for dramatic effect. Also: Emergency *lighting* torch.

flash: aberrant bright spot caused by unwanted reflection. Also: Very short *scene*. Also: Accidentally (or deliberately: see *flash frame*) *overexposed film frame*. Also: *Unprogrammed* news interruption.

flashback: interpolated "earlier" *scene*.

flash frame: *film frame* deliberately *overexposed* by cameraman as visual *editing cue*. Also produced by *pea bulb*.

flashlight (torch) battery: low-power traditional zinc shell containing carbon rod in magnesium paste. See: *dry cell*.

flash pan: in Britain, image-blurring *pan* shot, usually used for *transition*. Also called *whip* (*wizz*) pan.

flat: large framed-canvas or hardboard *set* piece (semi-permanent, light, moveable, self-supporting) for "walls" or vertical planes. Compare: *drop*. Also: Lacking in *video contrast*. Also: Without any *audio equalization*. Also: *Frequency response* of ±3 *db* from 50 to 14,000 *Hz*. Also: *Film projection* at 1.33:1 *aspect ratio*. Also: Television imaging techniques replacing *CRT* scansion with panel display.

flat screen: television picture concept utilizing plasma discharge; electroluminescent panels; *light-emitting diodes;* liquid crystals; electrochromic displays; etc., in place of *picture tube*.

Fletcher-Munson effect: tendency of human ear to "hear" less extreme *bass* and *treble* when *audio levels* are reduced. See: *middle range*.

flicker: *viewer* loss of *persistence of vision,* caused by *film projector* running too slow, or *shutter* malfunction.

flies: *studio* ceiling area for hoisted *luminaires* and *scenery* storage.

flighting: non-consecutive calendar periods of *broadcast* advertising. See: *cycle, hiatus*.

flip: change *art card* for camera. Also: *Optical* spin effect (called *flapover* in Britain). Also: Rotate *lens mount*.

flip cards: large "looseleaf" *art cards* carrying *program titles* or credits. See: *flip stand*. Compare: *crawl, draw cards*.

flippers—barn doors: adjustable metal side and/or top shades to narrow *luminaire beam.*

flippy disk: two-side *record*able *floppy disk.*

flip side: opposite side of *phonograph disk.*

flip stand: stand holding *flip cards* before camera for rapid, almost imperceptible downward "flipping."

FLIR—forward-looking infra-red: thermal video imaging system utilizing large matrix of discrete heat sensors and very high speed mechanical *scanning* system.

floodlight—flood: *unfocussed luminaire* (or *luminaire bank*) illuminating specific area without glare or shadow.

floor: television *set* or *studio* performance area.

floor manager: *director's* representative in charge of television *studio floor* activity, usually connected to *control room* by *headphones;* equivalent to theater stage manager.

floor men: television *production stagehands* or *grip crew.*

floor monitor: *playback monitor* for *cast/crew* reference.

floor plan: layout indication for *properties* and *scenery* for *studio* performance area. Compare: *light plot.*

floor secretary: in Britain, *continuity girl* on *production set.*

flop: reverse double-*sprocketed film* right for left.

floppy disk: flexible ($^1/_{16}''$ thick) one-side *video recording disk.*

flow: see *audience flow.*

fluff: performance speech error. Also: *Groove* dust gathered by *stylus.* Compare: *chip.*

fluroescence—luminescence: production of light (and heat) by energy absorption. Compare: *phosphoresence.*

fluorescent: tubular lamp emitting light from electrically-excited inner *phosphor* coating. Compare: *incandescent.*

fluorescent filter: *conversion filter* permitting use of *incandescent-* or daylight-*balanced film emulsion under fluorescent* (blue/green) illumination.

flutter: brief *tape speed* fluctuations, causing *audio* and/or *video* distortion. See: *time base connector.* Compare: *wow.*

flux: amount of light (measured in *lumens*). Also: Rate of energy transfer over a surface.

fly: suspend or store *scenery* over *set* by cable or rope. See: *flies.*

flyback: in Britain, *scanning beam* return to left side (or top) of television *picture tube* during *blanking interval.*

flying spot scanner: video-beam *transfer* technique, directly reading film surface (not a projection therefrom).

FM—frequency modulation: improved *audio rf transmission* technique utilizing one hundred (200 *KHz bandwidth*) *frequencies* from 88 to 108 *megahertz;* not subject to atmospheric and local *signal interference.* Called *VHF* in Britain. Compare: *AM.*

focal length: distance index—from optical center of a *lens* (at "infinity" setting) to *film emulsion* surface. 50mm *lens* is "normal" (similar to human vision field) for *35mm filming,* 25mm *lens* for *16mm filming.*

focal plane: plane passing at right angle through principal *focus* area of a *lens.* Compare *film plane.*

focal point: spot where *lens* (or reflector) concentrates all distant-source light rays.

focus: place an incoming *photon* at the point of a selected surface corresponding to the point in the field of vision from which the *photon* was reflected. Also: Bring *luminaire* or *electron beam* to a fine point.

focus control: television *picture gun* device for sharpest *beam scanning definition.*

focus group: selective research interview panel.

focus in (out): transitional *editing* device.

focus puller: in Britain, *assistant cameraman*—checking camera and *focus,* changing *lenses* and *magazines,* etc.

fog: spoil undeveloped *film* by accidental *exposure* to light. See: *changing bag, darkroom.*

fog filter: special *lens filter* affording softened photographic effect.

foldback: in Britain, *pre-recorded audio feed* to *studio loudspeaker.*

follow focus: alter camera *focus* on the move to hold subject in sharpest *definition.*

follow shot: camera move to *track* subject in motion.

follow spot: high-power, narrow-beam *spotlight* to track moving subject.

FOM—film operations manager: in Britain, liaison person between *BBC film* and *production* departments.

foot: end of *film* or *tape reel.* See: *tail.* Compare: *head.*

footage: (non-metric) standard *film* length measurement; sixteen *35mm,* forty *16mm* and 72 *Super 8mm frames* per *film foot.* Loosely, the *film* itself.

footage counter: direct *readout* indicator showing *raw stock* run through camera—or amount left in *magazine.* Also: Illuminated *mixing studio* indicator. Also: *Video tape* digital position index.

foot candle: older illumination standard (replaced by the modern *candela,* 1.02 foot candles) for photography and *projection;* amount of illumination received by a surface one foot from lighted "standard candle"; metric equivalent is *lux.*

footlambert: *luminance* measurement equal to reflection of one *lumen*—0.98 *foot candles* of light—covering a square foot of surface. Theatrical screen projection requires 10–12 footlamberts.

footprint: *satellite coverage* area.

force—push: develop *film emulsion* beyond recommended *exposure rating,* usually half or full *stop.*

foreground: part of *scene* nearest camera. Also: In Britain, call to clear area in front of camera during *rehearsal.*

foreground miniature: in Britain, obsolete technique (often involving painting on glass) preceding development of modern *optical film matteing.*

format: *radio station programming* concept. Also: *Program* styling. Also: Show *rundown* in order of appearance. Also: Screen proportions of projected picture.

Fortnightly Decision: 1968 Supreme Court ruling allowing *CATV* operators to take off the air and re-*transmit* television *programming* without regard to any copyright restrictions.

45 rpm—extended play: popular single-*cut phonograph disk* rotation speed.

four-framer—clip roll—pilots: in Britain, *laboratory film* test strips of *color balance* ranges prepared to determine final *printing light* selections.

four-H: in Britain, four-unit *video tape recording* (and *playback*) *headwheel*, rotating at right angles to transported *2" tape*, "writing" *video* information in successive almost-vertical stripes (1,2,3,4,1,2,3,4, etc.) Compare: *helical scan*.

Fourth Channel: unallocated (1978) British television transmission *frequency*.

four-way: in Britain, geared table device for *synchronously editing film* and *soundtrack*.

frame: individual *motion picture film* photograph—or the space it occupies; usually projected for $^{1}/_{24}$ second ($^{1}/_{25}$ second in Britain). Also: Register *film* in projector *gate*. Called *rack* in Britain. Also: Single $^{1}/_{30}$ second ($^{1}/_{25}$ second in Britain) television tube picture *scan* combining *interlaced* information (280,000 *pixels*) of two fields (262½ lines to a *field;* in Britain, 312½ lines). Also: All units included in a research sample—usually the telephone directory.

frame bar: see *frame line*.

frame cut: extraneous *frames* within a *scene* excised without evidence. Compare: *jump cut*.

frame frequency: number of *transmitted* television *frames per second;* 30 in U.S., 25 in Britain.

frame line—frame bar: thin horizontal line dividing *35 mm frames*.

frame glass—platen: optically clear hinged glass plate holding *cels* flat during *animation* photography.

frame grabber: *digital* storage *circuit* permitting *helical video tape freeze framing* without continuous *head*-to-*tape* contact.

frame memory: television *receiver circuitry* storing single *transmitted frame* for continuous *readout*.

framesnatch: *cable* television home control permitting *receiver* to "lock onto" one of 30 *completely different frames* specially *transmitted* each second, thus allowing *viewing*—for example—a miniaturized 30-page newspaper, one page at a time.

frames-per-second—fps: film *speed* through camera or *projector gate*. Compare: *ips*. Also: Television *transmission* standard; 30 in U.S., 25 in Britain.

frame-store: *analog*-to-*digital* television *signal* converter for storing thousands of pictures (*frames* or *stills*) on magnetic *disk packs* in minimum space. See: *ESS*.

frame up: adjust camera position for better composition. Also: Properly *register film* in projector *gate*.

framing: subject area included by camera *lens*.

franchise area: in Britain, *IBA*-company coverage area.

FRC—Federal Radio Commission: government agency set up under *Federal Radio Act* of 1927 to control U.S. *radio broadcasting;* replaced in 1934 by *FCC*.

freebie: something of value exchanged for media publicity. See: *junket, plugola*.

free-lance: self-employed individual.

free perspective: illusion of realistic dimension on a studio *set*.

freeze: agree on final *format*. Also: Completely forget one's lines. Called *dry* in Britain.

freeze frame—stop action: individual *film negative frame*, reprinted as continuous *positive* in middle of normal motion footage. Also: Identical visual effect achieved by *video tape disk recorder*.

Freeze Order: *FCC* television *station* application halt (September 30, 1948) to promulgate improved *transmission* standards.

French brace: swing-away permanently-attached hinged *scenery* support.

French flag: see *flag*.

French shoot: in Britain, seven continuous hours of production (from noon on) with no *break*.

French side—Radio Canada: Quebec French-language operation of the *CBC*.

frequency: rate at which electronic impulse or sound or light wave passes a given point in a specific time period (see: *amplitude, hertz, cps*); loosely, broadcast transmission *wavelength*. Also: Average count of times an audience is exposed to a *program* series or same *commercial* over specific number of weeks. See: *audience accumulation, impressions*. Compare: *reach*.

frequency discount—quantity discount: lower *station rate* available to advertisers scheduling *commercials* over 13-week *cycle* or multiples thereof—or at agreed minimum number of times each week. See: *rateholder*.

frequency equalizer—EQ: control device to improve *audio* quality, usually by suppressing one of the five *frequency* ranges.

frequency response: ability of equipment to *transmit* or reproduce varying frequencies of a *signal*.

fresnel: plano-convex *lens* thinned down in "stepped" form. Also: *Spotlight* with such *lens*.

friction head: rotating camera *mount* mechanically snubbed for smooth *panning* motion. See: *pan head*. Compare: *gear head*.

frilling: edge-loosening of *film emulsion* from *base*.

fringe area: outer reception limits of a broadcast *signal*.

fringe evening time: *broadcast* periods preceding or following *prime time;* i.e., Early (5:00 to 7:00 P.M.) and Late (11:00 P.M. to 1:00 A.M.). See: *time*.

fringing: multiple image mis-*registration*.

frocks: in Britain, performers' *wardrobe*.

from the top: *rehearsal* from very beginning of a performance.

front focus: *focus* a *zoom lens* in "in" position.

front porch: 1.59 *microsecond* interval between beginning of television *blanking retrace interval* and *synchronizing signal* that follows. Compare: *back porch, breezeway*.

front (axial) projection: scenic *background* effect, achieved by low-intensity *projection* of *location slides* or *film* along the taking-*lens* axis (by a 45° half-silvered mirror) directly on performers and on huge *Scotchlite* screen behind them. Called *reflex projection* in Britain. Compare: *background projector, rear screen projection, vizmo*.

FRP: see *SFP*.

frying pan: *set* screen to soften light source.

FS—full shot: performers and entire *background*. Compare: *LS, MS*.

f-stop: *aperture setting* indicating theoretical amount of light passing through *lens;* determined by dividing *focal length* by effective *diaphragm* diameter. Adjacent *f-stop* numbers double (or halve) amount of transmitted light. See: *f, stop*. Compare: *T-stop*.

FTC—Federal Trade Commission: government agency charged with advertising regulation. Compare: *FCC*.

F-2: *ionospheric* layer creating heavy 10-40 *MHz radio wave* reflection when subjected to *sunspot ionization*.

fuff: in Britain, plastic snow flakes.

full coat: *35mm sprocket-holed film* completely coated one side with metallic *oxide* for multiple-track *magnetic recording*. Called *full stripe* in Britain. (When used for single-track recording, U.S. practice is to record down edge; Britain uses 200 mil center path.)

fuller's earth: mineral powder simulating *set* "dust."

full net: all-*affiliate network hookup*. Called *all* in Britain.

full network station: *affiliate* carrying at least 85% of *network prime time programming*.

full track: *recording* on all the available *audio tape surface*. Compare: *half track*.

funnel—snoot: conelike or tubelike attachment pinpointing *spotlight beam*.

funny paper effect: electronic offset of *chrominance* and *luminance signals* in a television picture.

FV: see *Family Viewing Time*.

FX: extraneous effects. Compare: *SFX*.

FYI—for your information: routing notation.

G

GAC: in Britain, General Advisory Councils providing both *BBC* and *IBA* with public input.

gaffer: chief *set* electrician. See: *sparks*.

gaffer grip—gator grip—bear trap: heavy-duty *set* spring clamp, often with *luminaire* mount.

gaffer tape: strong, extremely adhesive aluminized-surface pressure-sensitive tape for temporary *set* or *location* rigging.

gain: *audio* amplification, usually expressed in *decibels*. Also: *Video contrast* ratio. See: *black level, reference white*.

gallery—box: in Britain, small room for *production* management, usually higher than performing *studio* and separated from it by soundproof window and "sound lock."

game: see *video game*.

game show: television giveaway *program* with host and elaborate questioning and scoring *props*.

gamma: *contrast* characteristics of developed *film*. Also: Television camera *input/output contrast* ratio.

gang: two or more switches on single control.

gantry: in Britain, peripheral walkway affording access to *runners*.

gap: microscopic space (1/10,000–1/20,000 inch) between two poles of magnetic *recording, playback* or *erase head*.

garbage: *rf* spillover *interference* onto adjacent *frequencies*.

gas: pressurize a camera *boom* tank.

gash: in Britain, worthless *film*.

gate: (picture gate) camera or *projector* opening in which each *frame* is held momentarily for exposure or projection; (sound gate) *projector* mechanism "reading" *optical sound-track*.

gator grip—gaffer grip—bear trap: heavy-duty *set* spring clamp, often with *luminaire* mount.

gauss: (after propounder of mathematical theory of electricity) unit of magnetic *induction*.

gauze: light *diffuser*. See: *spun, butterfly*.

G clamp: (British) see *C clamp*.

gear head: hand-operated camera *mount* with gear wheels controlling *pan/tilt* movement. See: *cradle head*. Compare: *friction head*.

gel(atin): translucent celluloid-like *filter* altering color characteristics of a light source. See: *color media*. Called *jelly* in Britain.

Gemini: (obsolete) simultaneous *video tape*-and-*16mm film* recording system, developed as an *editing* technique.

generating element: *microphone transducer*.

generation: *duplication* stage. "First generation" is original material; "second" is its duplicate; "third" is a duplicate of the second; etc. Each generation represents some loss of quality.

generator: portable gasoline- or diesel-powered dynamo generating alternating current (*AC*). Called *alternator* in Britain.

generator truck: conveyance for above.

generic: in Britain, *on-air* promotional material for television series.

genlock: device synchronizing television *signal* sources.

geometry errors: *video tape velocity* and *time base* dimensional changes.

geosynchronous: orbital television *satellite* moving at speed of earth's rotation (thus "standing still").

get out: in Britain, time required to *strike* a *set*.

Gev: one billion electron-*volts*. Compare: *mev*.

ghost: offset secondary *picture tube* image, caused by reflected (earlier or later) television *transmission signal*. See: *multipath*.

ghoster: in Britain, overtime *production* beyond 1:00 A.M.

Gibson Girl: obsolete *audio tape splicer* design. Compare: *splicing block*.

gigahertz—GHz: one billion *hertz*.

gigawatt—GW: one billion *watts;* one million *kW*.

gimmick: trick or device.

giraffe: in Britain, small *microphone boom*.

glass shot: obsolete technique—painting on glass—that preceded development of modern optical *film matteing*. Also: Package, etc., affixed to *limbo* sheet of glass.

glitch: random television *picture noise* appearing as ascending horizontal bar.

glossy: shiny-finished photographic print.

GMT—Greenwich Mean Time: mean solar time at Greenwich, England meridian.

gobo: sound-absorbing material or screen. Also: Opaque shape to screen a *set* light. See: *finger, flag, cutter, dot, mask*. Also: In Britain, a *cookie*.

Godslot: (now discontinued) statutory British Sunday evening religious hour. Formally called *closed period*.

golden time: Sunday, holiday or other special overtime, compensated under union agreements at more than normal (1½ ×) overtime rate.

gooseneck: bendable *microphone* stand.

gopher: *production* assistant who "goes for" coffee, etc.

go to black: fade from *image* to blank screen.

GRA—Granada: one of British *IBA's "Big Five"* (the *Central Companies*).

grad: in Britain, partial *neutral density filter*.

grading: in Britain, subjective alteration of *printing light intensities* and *color filters* to achieve a *balanced film positive* from *unbalanced negative* material.

grading print: in Britain, initial *married* evaluation *film print* from completed *picture* and *track negative*. Compare: *double head, show print*.

grain: molecular *film emulsion* structure.

Grammy: (from *gramaphone*) annual U.S. recording industry award.

gramophone: in Britain, *audio disk* player.

grating: in Britain, television camera *alignment* pattern.

gray scale: ten-step intensity scale evaluating *shading* of black-and-white television picture. [Note: Nos. 1 (high, pure white) and 10 (low, pure black) cannot be adequately reproduced by a television *picture tube*.] See: *contrast range*.

green print: newly-made *positive* on which *emulsion* may still be soft, affecting *focus*.

green room: performers' lounge.

greensmen: studio *crew* handling *set* foliage.

grid(iron): metal girders or pipr latticework suspending *luminaires,* etc. over *set*. Called *runners* in Britain. See: *catwalk*. Also: **grid:** television camera *alignment* chart. Called *grating* in Britain. Compare: *chip chart*. Also: Wire mesh *vacuum tube* element.

grille cloth: *loudspeaker* covering.

grip: *set* worker charged with lifting, carrying or pushing.

groove: see *microgroove*.

gross rating points—GRP: total number of *rating points* for specific television advertising *schedule,* prepared without regard to viewer *duplication*. Compare: *net rating points*.

Groucho: in Britain, performer's *floor mark*.

ground: zero *voltage* point in an electrical system. Called *earth* in Britain.

ground glass: translucent glass screen on which *viewfinder* image is *focussed*.

ground row—cove: *cyc* baseboard (usually concealing *luminaire strip*).

groundwave: primary portion of *broadcast signal* following ground contour. Compare: *sky wave*.

guard band: separating section of *audio* or *video tape* between different *recorded tracks*.

guide track—scratch track: temporary *soundtrack* prepared to assist *editing* or subsequent *silent* camera work.

guillotine splicer: *film editing* device using continuous roll of pressure-sensitive tape applied across the *film,* punch-perforated and trimmed on both sides by knives.

gun: television *cathode ray tube* source continuously emitting narrow *focusable beam* of electrons.

H

HAAT: height of *transmission antenna* above average terrain.

half apple: rugged low wooden box used on *set* to raise apparent height of performers or *props*. See: *apple*.

half broad: box-shaped 1,000-*watt floodlight*. See: *broad*.

half track: reversible *audio recording tape* with *signal* on top 40% only. Compare: *full track*. Also: Combination of *optical* and *magnetic sound tracks* on single *film print*.

halide: binary compound containing one of the halogens: chlorine, bromine, flourine, iodine. See: *tungsten-halogen*.

halo—halation: dark television *picture tube* area *ringing* an *overloaded* bright area. Also: *Print flare* caused by excessive light bouncing back through *emulsion* from *film base*.

ham: amateur *short wave radio* operator.

hammock: unpopular *network* position between two popular programs.

hand-held: without camera *tripod* or *dolly*—or *microphone* support. See: *enhanced hand-held*.

hand model: performer using hands (only) in *frame*.

handout: publicity *release* provided by subject.

hand props: small personal *properties*.

happy talk: inconsequential television news *programming*.

hard: high in *contrast*.

hard copy: paper *CRT* printout. Compare: *soft copy*.

harden: sharpen *focus*. Compare: *soft*.

Hard Rock: *Variety's* epithet for New York corporate headquarters of *American Broadcasting Companies*, matching *Thirty Rock* (*NBC*) and *Black Rock* (*CBS*).

hardware: electronic equipment used to present *broadcast program* material (*software*).

harmonic: *signal* whose *frequency* is an integral multiple of the fundamental *frequency* from which it is derived or related.

harmonic distortion: addition of spurious *frequencies* as integer multiples of input signal.

harness: grouped and tied wires or *cables*.

haze filter: *lens filter* removing some ultraviolet and blue light and reducing effect of atmospheric haze.

Hazeltine: electro-optical *negative color film* analyzer determining proper *printing exposures*.

HBO—Home Box Office: Time/Life *cable* casting subsidiary.

head: beginning of *reel* of *tape* or *film*. Compare: *tail*. Also: *Tape recording* or *playback transducer*. Also: *Picture* or *sound gate* on *film editing* machine; *sound gate* on *film projector*. Also: Camera mount on *tripod, dolly* or *boom*.

head alignment: magnetic *head* adjustment for maximized *recording* or *playback* characteristics. See: *bias*.

head end: *antenna*/equipment origination point for *cable* television *transmission*.

header: in Britain, short opening sequence in advance of television *program main title*.

headlife: nominal *video recording head* overhaul-to-overhaul period.

headphones: tiny wired *speakers* worn over each ear. Compare: *earphone, headset*.

headroom: space between top of framed object and top edge of *frame*.

headset: *intercom* or *PL* station consisting of headband-mounted earpiece-and-mouthpiece. Compare: *headphones*.

headsheet: *talent* photograph. Compare: *composite*.

head shot: *framing* performer's head and shoulders.

heads out: *film* (or *tape*) *reel* ready for *projection* (or *playback*). Compare: *tails out*.

headwheel: rotating magnets of *quad video tape record/playback* assembly.

heaviside layer: (after British physicist who discovered it, 1902) *ionosphere,* 25 to 250 miles high, "bouncing" *radio* waves back to earth for wider *signal coverage.* Compare: *troposphere.*

hectohertz: 100 *hertz.*

height: vertical size of television picture. Compare: *width.*

helical scan (slant track): *video tape* equipment with one or two *recording heads* "writing" *video* information horizontally in long parallel slants across *tape* "wrapped" in a helix. Uniquely offers a *still* picture, but is more susceptible than *quadruplex* to *tape* stretch and slippage. Developed in 1965, first used in miniaturized *video tape recording* systems.

helios noise: five-minute all-wave *interference* when *satellite* passes between sun and *tracking earth station.*

henry: (after the electromagnetic pioneer) unit of *inductance.*

hertz—Hz: (after the discoverer of *electromagnetic* or *radio waves*) *frequency* unit equal to one *cycle per second.* Male voice range is 500–800 *Hz;* female, 1,000–2,000 *Hz.* "Hi-fi" is 20–20,000 *Hz;* human audibility range is usually 50–15,000 *Hz.*

hessian: in Britain, coarse *set drape* cloth material.

HFR—hold for release: pending *air* material.

hiatus: planned interruption of *commercial broadcast schedule,* usually to extend an advertising budget. See: *cycle, flighting.*

HID—high-intensity discharge: mercury, *metal halide* and high-pressure sodium *lamps.*

hidden camera: impromptu television interview technique, usually *pre-recorded.*

hi-fi—high-fidelity: sonic reproduction characterized by uniform *frequency response* (less than 3 *db* deviation from 20 to 20,000 *Hz*), low *distortion* (less than 0.5%) and low extraneous *noise* (at least 50 *db* below *signal*).

high band: improved *video tape recording* technique utilizing the 7.1 to 10 *megahertz band* for improved *signal-to-noise* *ratio;* or, equipment for such *recording.* (Note: *LOW-band video tapes* can be *played back* on *high-band* equipment.)

high con(trast): special *film* used in *optical printing* to drop out any *emulsion* background from *titling mattes,* etc.

high-energy: tape requiring stronger magnetic recording field strength (improving *signal-to-noise ratio*).

high hat—top hat: *tripod* extension for high camera angles; also used by itself for low camera angles.

high gain—high level: *signal level* of one *volt* or more. Compare: *low gain.*

high key: bright illumination emphasizing the upper *gray scale,* producing few or no dark areas. Compare: *low key.*

highlight: maximum *brightness* of a positive *image.*

highs—high frequencies: sound *frequencies* around 15,000 *hertz.* Compare: *lows, middle range.*

high-speed duplication: *re-recording* one or more copies from a *tape master* at a speed many times faster than the original *recording.*

high-speed photography: special *film* cameras offering *exposure* rates from 25 to 30,000,000 *frames per second.* Called *fast motion* in Britain.

high Z: see *Z.*

hiss: aberrant *high-frequency* recorded signals audible during tape playback.

hit: undesirable brief, distinctive *audio* noise. Also: Sudden *effect.*

Hitachi: major Japanese electronics manufacturer.

hit the mark: move to a pre-determined *set* point. Compare: *miss the mark.*

hitchhike: *sponsor announcement* following *program's* actual end. Compare: *cowcatcher, billboard.*

Ho Chi Minh Trail: in Britain, unorthodox path around *production* difficulty.

hold: any *cel* in multi-layered *animation* photography not changed from *frame* to *frame.* Also: Repetitive *printing* of single *live-action frame.* Also: Successful *tape* performance held for review before final selection. See: *buy.* Also: Tentative performer *booking.* Compare: *audition.*

holding fee: scheduled payment to *commercial* talent between *cycles* of actual *air* use.

hologram—holography: *laser*-produced "three-dimensional" image. See: *wave-front reconstruction*.

holy factor: *high-key* illumination for color photography.

homes: basic audience survey count of households owning one or more *broadcast receivers*.

hooking: television picture *distortion* caused by incorrect *video tape/playback head* timing coordination. See: *bending, flagging*.

hookup: *circuit* connection. Also: Loosely, multi-*station program* interconnection. Also: First and last interchangeable *cels* of *animation cycle*.

Hooper(ating): radio audience telephone survey service. Sold to A. C. *Nielsen* in 1950's.

horizontal: television *scan line signal*, requiring 0.4 *nanosecond* stability.

horizontal blanking: *signal* suppression during horizontal *retrace*.

horizontal polarization: original television *signal transmission* pattern—along horizontal plane—subject to *ghosting*. Compare: *circular polarization*.

horizontal resolution: camera ability (expressed in "lines") to detect *intensity* changes along a single *scan line*. See: *pixel*. Compare: *vertical resolution*.

horizontal saturation: heavy *broadcast* advertising *schedule* using same *time* period for several consecutive days. Compare: *roadblocking, vertical saturation*.

horse: in Britain, *film editing feed reel* stand.

hot: extremely bright *image*. Also: Energized equipment or *circuit*. See: *live*. Compare: *dead*.

hot press: *title card* imprinting technique utilizing highly reflective colored foil in place of ink.

hot spot: excessive reflection from part of illuminated object.

hour meter: digital counter measuring equipment's elapsed operating time (for maintenance scheduling).

house agency: *agency* function partially or fully controlled by advertising *client*.

housecleaning: sweeping personnel replacement.

(TV) household: one of 65 million homes in the U.S. with television *receivers*. Compare: *radio home*.

housewife: in audience surveys, any female head of a household aged 16+.

housewife time—daytime: broadcast *time* sale classification: 10:00 A.M. to 4:00 P.M. See: *time*.

housing: equipment shell.

hue: distinctive color *wavelength* (black, gray and white have no *hue*). See: *chroma, intensity*. Compare: *saturation*.

hum: undesirable *low-frequency* note caused by improper *circuit alignment*.

hum bars—venetian blind effect: 60 *Hz interference*, creating broad moving or stationary horizontal *picture* bars.

hunting: equipment failure to maintain correct *speed*.

HUR—homes using radio: audience survey count of *broadcast homes* listening to *radio* during average quarter-hour *time* period. See: *audience potential*.

HUT—homes using TV: audience survey count of *broadcast homes* viewing television during average quarter-hour *time* period. See: *audience potential*.

hyperfocal: distance between *lens* at *infinity* setting and nearest object in acceptable *focus*.

hypo—sodium thiosulfate: photo-developing fixative. Also: **hypo:** schedule highly popular *programming* during *station rating* periods. See: *rating book*.

Hz: see *hertz*.

I

IATSE—International Alliance of Theatrical Stage Employees: *set* workers' union.

IBA—Independent Broadcasting Authority: organization (until 1972, ITA—Independent Television Authority) established under 1964 Television Act to supervise Britain's *commercial broadcasting;* consists of fifteen *program contractors* (see *Big Five*) supplying regional *transmitters*. See: *ICTA*.

IBEW—International Brotherhood of Electrical Workers: *broadcast* technicians' union.

IC—integrated circuit: encapsulated *semi-conductor chip* affixed to tiny *dialectric* base, performing control function. See: *microprocessor*.

iconoscope: (coined by inventor Zworykin—from Russian "holy image") early television camera *pickup tube* (1923).

ICTA—Independent Television Companies Association: Britain's 15-*IBA*-member trade association. Compare: *NAB*.

ID—station identification: formerly *10-second commercial* announcement with *audio* limited to 8 seconds or less to allow for shared *station identification;* now any *10-second spot*.

ident board: see *number board*.

idiot card: off-camera *cue card* in performer's view. Compare: *prompter*.

IEEE—Institute of Electrical and Electronic Engineers: British standard-setting professional engineering group. Compare: *SMPTE*.

if—intermediate frequency: standard (41–47 *MHz*) *frequency* for television *signal* path within *receiver*. Compare: *rf*.

Ikegami: Japanese electronics firm manufacturing *hand-held* television cameras. See: *ENG*.

ILR: in Britain, *I*ndependent *L*ocal *R*adio corporations.

image: *film* or television picture.

image dissector: see *dissector*.

image enhancer: television *signal* processor creating a "crisper" picture by "filling in" missing *luminance* detail.

image intensifier: electronic *lens* adapter improving low light *levels* by using *fiber optics* to break up *image* into series of *amplified* points.

image isocon: sensitive *camera pickup tube* designed for low light *levels*. Compare: *SEC, SIT*.

image orthicon—I.O.: older type of sensitive (15–20:1 *contrast range*) television camera *pickup tube;* origin of "*Emmy* (immy) Award" epithet originated by Henry R. Lubcke (1948). Compare: *Plumbicon, saticon, vidicon*.

image pickup tube: see *camera tube*.

image retention—lag: two (or more) *frame* "ghosting" behind fast-moving television camera subjects, caused by insufficient illumination (accentuated in low *field*-per-second systems). Eliminated in *solid-state* cameras. See: *bias light*. Compare: *comet tail*.

Image Transform: proprietary computerized high-quality *video tape*-to-*film transfer* system.

imbibition: final *dye transfer* stage of *Technicolor printing* process.

impedance: apparent *AC resistance* corresponding to actual *DC resistance*. Measured in *ohms*. Symbol: *Z*.

imported signal—distant signal: cable television *programming* taken off *air* outside the system's normal reception area and forwarded for local distribution.

impressions: gross (duplicated) *program* or *commercial* audience. See: *audience accumulation*.

in: movement towards. Compare: *out*.

in-betweens: sequential *animation* drawings between *extremes*. Compare: *animation design*.

incandescent: inert-gas-filled electric lamp (invented 1879) emitting light (and heat) from an excited *tungsten filament*. Compare: *fluorescent*.

inching knob: *editor/projector* control moving *film* one *frame* at a time.

incident: light striking subject from any source.

inclining prism: rotating *viewfinder* permitting viewing at awkward camera angles.

in-cue: opening words of *cue* line. Compare: *out-cue*.

independent—"indie"—"indy": commercially operated *broadcast station* carrying less than 10 hours of *network programming* a week; 16% of all television *stations* (1978). Compare: *affiliate, O & O's*.

inductance: electric energy storage in a magnetic field, generated by current flow in *conductor*, measured in *henrys*. Compare: *capacitance*.

induction: transmission of electric or magnetic *currents* without direct *connection*.

industrial: media selling industrial as opposed to consumer products.

infinity: distance from *lens*—often not more than thirty feet—beyond which camera sees all light rays as parallel.

infra-red: *emulsion* sensitive to light waves longer than visible red. Compare: *actinic light*.

infrasonic: below audible (20 *Hz*-up) range. Compare: *sonic, ultrasonic*.

ink-and-paint: completion stage after *pencil test* of full *animation*.

inky—inky dink: tiny 100-to-250 *watt fresnel spotlight*.

inlay: see *chromakey*.

in phase: perfect coordination of *film* movement through *gate*, with rotation of camera *shutter*. Also: Any electronic *synchronization*.

input: incoming power or *signal* (or equipment *terminal* receiving it).

insert: portion *matted* into larger television *picture*. Also: Additional *video tape* or *film* added into previously completed material. Compare: *assemble*. Also: *Close-up* of inanimate object. See: *table top*.

insert camera: small television camera for *superimposing* artwork, *titles,* etc. Called *caption scanner* in Britain.

insertion: individual *commercial* appearance on *broadcast* advertising *schedule*.

insertion loss: *signal* strength decrease when piece of equipment is inserted into *circuit*.

insert stage: small *studio* for minor (*table top*) photography.

in shot—in frame: accidental visual intrusion.

instantlies: *video tape "dailies"*.

instant replay: immediate *playback* (often *slow motion* and *freeze frame*) from *video disk recording* of ongoing *live telecast* (usually sports). See: *isolated*.

insulation: *dialectric* protective covering on wire or *cable*.

insurance—cover shot: wide camera position, *protection* for *jump cut lip sync close-ups*. Compare: *cutaway*.

in sync: *sound* and *picture* elements exactly *aligned*.

int.—interior: an indoor *set*. Compare: *ext*.

integrated: *commercial* advertising format, claiming (somewhat arbitrarily) a relationship between two (or more) products made by different corporate advertisers, thus obtaining lowered pro-rata *time* charges. Compare: *piggyback*. Also: Cast-delivered *commercial* within program format.

integrated circuit—IC: encapsulated *semi-conductor chip* affixed to tiny *dialectric* base, performing control function. See: *microprocessor*.

integration: *editing commercials* into body of recorded (*film* or *tape*) television *program*.

INTELSAT—International Telecommunications Satellite Organization: global communications *satellite* system established in 1964, now including more than 94 shareholding nations with five *satellites* and 133 *earth stations*. U.S. (*Comsat*) share = more than 30%. Various *Intelsat satellites* in 6,830 mph *geosynchronous* orbits 22,240 miles above

Atlantic, Pacific and Indian Oceans can carry 9,000 *audio channels* or 12 high-grade (or 24 low-grade) television *video/audio channels.*

intensity—chroma: measure of color *hue* and *saturation* (undiluted with white, black or gray). Also: **intensity:** strength of a light or sound wave, usually measured by its *amplitude.* Also: Strength of a light source in a particular direction, measured in *candelas.*

intercom: local voice communication system. See: *headset.* Compare: *PL.*

intercut: rapid picture-to-picture alteration. Called *crosscut* in Britain. Compare: *dissolve.*

interface: connection of compatible equipment. Compare: *noncompatibility.*

interference: extraneous electronic impulses disrupting normal *signal transmission.*

interlace: sequential *scanning* of alternate lines on television tube to create a "complete" *picture* in two passes of 262½ *lines* each; reduces *flicker* potential. See: *positive interlace, random interlace.*

interlock: separated but *synchronized film work picture* and magnetic *soundtrack.* Compare: *composite.* Also: System for projecting above. Called *double head* in Britain.

intermediate: *reversal* color *film* for making *opticals* or *duplicates.*

intermediate film process: Baird's pioneering *BBC* television camera technique (1936) utilizing 17.5mm *film* and 67-second-delayed *sound* and 240-line mechanical *disk scanning.* Replaced (1937) by EMI instantaneous 405-line electronic *scanning.*

intermittent shutter: rotating prismatic *lens* arrangement replacing normal camera *shutter.* Compare: *mirror shutter.*

intermodulation distortion—IM: generation of spurious *frequencies* during *signal* processing.

internal delay: length of time of *signal* passage through equipment.

internegative: *finegrain optical color negative* struck from original *reversal* or *interpositive* materials; used for *release printing.*

interpositive—IP: *finegrain color positive* struck from a selected section of original camera *negative;* used to make *internegative*.

Intersync: *video tape recording* accessory equipment *synchronizing signals* of *recorders* and *live* cameras.

intervalometer: automatic motion picture camera *shutter*-tripping device, adjustable to various time lapses.

Intervision: East European television *network*.

in the can: recorded *broadcast* material complete and ready for *air*.

inverter: *DC* to *AC* conversion device. Compare: *rectifier*.

ion: atom with net *positive* charge due to (*negative*) electron loss.

ionization: atomic electron loss created by application of energy.

ionized: *positively* charged.

ionosphere: atmospheric band 25 to 250 miles high, "bouncing" *radio waves* up to 30 *MHz* back to earth for wider *signal* coverage. Compare: *troposphere*. See: *heaviside layer, skywave*.

ion trap: magnetic field/*aperture* passing electron *beams* but blocking *ions*.

IPA—Institute of Practitioners in Advertising: British agency group exchanging information and establishing general policy and industry standards. Compare: *AA, AAAA, Advertising Council, ANA, ISBA, NA(RT)B*.

ips—inches-per-second: *tape* travel *speed* measurement. Compare: *frames-per-second*.

iris: *wipe* (in or out) *effect*, generated by a circle.

iris—diaphragm: adjustable *aperture* of overlapping metal leaves controlling amount of light passing through *lens*. See: *stop*.

IRN—Independent Radio News: Britain's *commercial radio* newsgathering organization.

IRTS—International Radio & Television Society: membership group of *broadcast* professionals.

ISBA—Incorporated Society of British Advertisers: client group exchanging information and establishing general policy and industry standards. Compare: *AA, AAAA, Advertising Council, ANA, IPA, NA(TR)B*.

I signal ("in phase" signal): orange-to-*cyan chrominance side-*

band (3.58 *MHz*) produced by *subcarrier modulation* phased 57° from *color burst* reference. See: *Q signal*. Compare: *Y signal*.

island: group of television *station film* and *slide projectors* feeding a *camera chain*.

island position: *commercial* isolated by *program* material from any other television advertising.

isolated: camera feeding *instant replay* action only.

ITA: see *IBA*.

I.T. band: European *M & E*.

ITFS—Instructional Fixed Television Service: school (only) *broadcasting* service (around 2,500 *MHz*).

ITN—Independent Television News: Britain's jointly-*IBS*-owned *broadcast* news gathering organization.

ITU—International Telecommunications Union: United Nations *broadcast* agency.

J

jack: plug-in electronic *connection*.

jackfield: in Britain, temporary *circuit connectors,* often replaced by *switcher*.

jack tube—polecat: telescopic *luminaire* support braced between walls.

jam: *film* camera pile-up. See: *bird's nest, buckle*.

jelly: in Britain, translucent celluloid-like *filter* to alter color characteristics of a light source. See: *color media*.

jenny: power *generator*.

jib: in Britain, cantilevered camera *mount* of varying size and length.

JICRAR—Joint Industry Committee for Radio Audience Research: British *AGB* group compiling weekly radio audience reports. Compare: *JICTAR, RADAR*.

JICTAR—Joint Industry Committee for Television Advertising Research: British *AGB* group compiling weekly television audience reports. Compare: *JICRAR*.

jingle: musical *broadcast* advertisement, usually sung.

jitter: small, rapid *signal amplitude* or *phase* instability.

jog: *frame*-by-*frame video tape* movement during *helical scan editing*.

joiner: in Britain, device for accurately *splicing edited film frames* with transparent tape or *cement*.

jolly: in Britain, materials used to spread or soften illumination.

Jones plug: polarized multi-*connector*.

joystick: hand control for remote operation of equipment.

judder: in Britain, violent vertical *picture* unsteadiness.

judgment sample: research units subjectively selected for statistical projection.

juice: electric *current*.

jump cut: poor *edit* of interrupted subject movement. See: *frame cut*. Compare: *jump cut, match cut*.

jumper: power *cable* extension.

jump out: remove extraneous *frames* within a scene without visual evidence. Compare: *frame cut, jump cut*.

junction box: portable *set* terminal for power *cables*. See: *spider*.

junior: 2,000-*watt spotlight*. Also called *two* or *2K*. Compare: *senior*.

junk: inoperative *satellites* still in orbit.

junk—dump: destroy.

junket: expense-paid trip exchanged for media publicity. See: *freebie*. Compare: *payola, plugola*.

JVC—Japan Victor Corporation: major Japanese electronics manufacturer.

JWT—J. Walter Thompson: major advertising agency.

K

K: see *kilowatt*.

°K—degrees Kelvin: measurement of light source *color temperature*. $0\,°K$ is $-273.16°$ C; each $°K = 1°$ C.

KDKA: first U.S. commercial *broadcasting station* (Pittsburgh, November, 1920).

Kem: horizontal *film*-and-*sound editing machine*. See: *Steenbeck, Moviola*.

key in: *matte* an image electronically. See: *plate*.

key (light): apparent principal light source modeling a subject with shadows and form; usually a single front *spotlight* placed first. Compare: *ambient, fill light, backlight, rimlight*.

key number: in Britain, multi-digit identification number applied on each foot of *negative raw stock*.

keys: in Britain, important change-of-action drawings in an *animation* sequence.

keystone: *distortion* caused by incorrect *projector*-to-*screen* angle.

kicker: light striking back and side of subject. Compare: *key*.

kidvid: television *programming* for children.

kill: extinguish or eliminate.

kilocycle—kC: *frequency* unit equal to 1,000 *cycles-per-second;* now called *kilohertz* (*kH*).

kilohertz—kH—kHz: (see above; renamed after discoverer of electromagnetic or *radio* waves) one thousand *hertz. AM* *radio* operates from 550 to 1,600 *kHz* (*FM radio* operates from 88 to 108 *MHz*).

kilowatt—kW—K: 1,000 *watts*.

kinescope—kine: poor-quality direct *reversal motion picture film recording* of television *tube picture,* first developed by Hartley and Ives in 1927. Also called *telerecording* (*TVR*).

kinetograph: *motion picture* strip *film* machine (Edison, 1889).

Kinetoscope (later **Cinématographe**): early *motion picture projector* (Lumière Brothers, 1895).

klystron: *vacuum tube* generating *ultra high frequency radio waves.*

knee: characteristic shape of *image orthicon tube* light pickup curve.

knock-out tabs: pair of easily-removed "wings" on *audio cassette* back; removing either one deactivates *re-record* capability of that *half track.* Compare: *record button.*

knuckle—clamping disk: adjustable *century stand* head, grooved to accept pipe *booms, flag* stems, etc.

Kodak Special: in Britain, spurious photography with a purposely-empty camera.

L

lab(oratory): facility for *developing* and *printing exposed film*.

lace—lace up: *thread film* into a *projection path*.

lag—image retention: two (or more) *frame* "ghosting" behind fast-moving television camera subjects, caused by insufficient illumination (accentuated in low *field*-per-second television systems). Eliminated by *solid-state* cameras. See: *bias light*. Compare: *comet tail*.

lambert: light *reflectance* measurement unit = 1 *lumen* per cm².

lamp: light-producing device. Compare: *bulb*.

lamp lumens: total amount of light available from *lamp*.

land line: *cable transmission*.

lap: cross-*dissolve* into new material while *dissolving* out of old.

lapel mike: *microphone* clipped to clothing. Compare *lavalier*.

lap switch: imperceptible *dissolve* between two video *signals,* in about 15–20 *milliseconds*.

laser: (from *L*ight *A*mplification by *S*timulated *E*mission of *R*adiation) device generating long, narrow beam of visible electromagnetic waves (in *picosecond pulses*), from 80 to 1,000 *terahertz*. Ruby laser developed by Gould in 1957, based on (1917) Einstein theory. Also: *Videotape-to-film transfer* technique (using three laser beams, one for each color). Compare: *Vidtronics*. Also: *Video disk recording* technique.

latent: *exposed* but un*developed film image*.

latitude: proper combinations of *shutter* speed and *lens aperture* to expose a particular *film emulsion* (faster *emulsions* offer wider latitudes).

laugh track: *pre-recorded* joke responses.

lavalier(e): *microphone* hung around the neck, leaving performer's hands free. Compare: *lapel mike.*

lavender: in Britain, colored-netting light *diffuser.* Also: Obsolete *positive film duping stock.*

lay: in Britain, *synchronize* track(s) to a *picture.*

lay an egg: fail in performance.

layout: *animator's* guide for plotting *film action.* Also: Editorial plan for *optical* cameraman.

lazy arm: in Britain, small *microphone boom.*

LCU—large close-up: in Britain, performer's features. Also called *big close-up (BCU).*

L cut: *VTR* edit to new *picture* with no change in *audio* source.

lead: principal role. Also: Wired *connection.*

lead acid accumulator: traditional rechargeable sulfuric acid *storage battery.* Compare: *dry cell.*

leader: non-projected identification and *audio* and/or *video* timing *countdown* at head of *film* or *video tape,* for exact cueing purposes. See: *video leader.* Also: *Head* or *tail* portion of *film* or *tape* "*leading*" it from *feed* to *take-up reels* through *projection* or *playback path.* Also: Blank opaque film (black or white) spliced as spacing between sections of *workprint footage;* called *build up* in Britain. Also: Paper or plastic *audio tape* "spacing."

lead-in: cast introduction to program *commercial.* Also: *Program* preceding.

lead-out: *program* following.

lead oxide tube: improved television camera *pickup tube* with lead oxide *target,* offering high sensitivity, low *dark current,* 1-*gamma,* low *lag,* uniform *shading* and temperature stability. See: *Plumbicon.*

lead sheet: horizontal "bar graph" showing exact relationship of *animation* action to music beats and voice syllables. Also: Complete *score* of a musical accompaniment.

lead time: period between a system's research and development, and its initial marketing.

LED—light-emitting diode: glowing crystal *chip semi-conductor*. 150,000 *LED's* (one for each *pixel*) can create a wall-sized television *screen*.

leg: *network* interconnection between regional *affiliate stations*.

lens: glass optical system focusing light rays to form an image.

lens adapter: camera device permitting easy *lens* interchange.

lens cap: protective dust (and light) cover. See: *cap up*.

lens extender: device to hold *lens* away from camera for *close-up* photography. See: *diopter lens, extension tube, proxar*.

lens hood: tunnel-shaped camera attachment blocking extraneous light sources. See: *matte box*.

lens prism: multiple-image attachment.

lens speed: light transmission capability (function of *focal length* to diameter); *faster lenses* have lower *f-stop* numbers.

lens turret: old rotatable television camera *mount* holding up to five lenses; obsoleted by *zoom lens*.

lettering safety: *picture tube* area within which *transmitted titling* is safely clear of *masks* on even slightly *overscanned receivers*. Compare: *cut off, picture safety*.

letter of adherence: document establishing contractual obligation of hiring *producer* to U.S. *talent* unions. See: *signatory*.

level: *audio* or *video amplitude* or *intensity*. Also: *Rehearsal* test of that *intensity*.

level cut: see *level sync*.

level distortion: improper changes in television *picture* color *saturation* and *intensity*.

level sync(hronization): in Britain, *frame-to-frame synchronization* of *work picture* and *soundtrack*, with no allowance for *film pullup*. See: *cutting sync*.

lexicographer: a harmless *drudge* that busies himself detailing the origin and signification of words.

library footage—stock shot: previously photographed *film footage* licensed for re-use. See: *scratch print*.

library music—stock music: previously *recorded background* music *licensed* for re-use. See: *needle drop*.

license: *FCC* permission to operate a *broadcast* facility. In Britain, permission from Minister of Posts and Communications to operate a *broadcast receiver*. Also: Music performance permission.

lift: material from earlier and/or longer *production*.

lifter: *audio recorder* device removing *tape* from close *head* contact during *fast forward* or *rewind*.

light: visible electromagnetic radiant energy in *wavelengths* between 400 and 750 *millimicrons*.

light box: illuminated translucent (rotating) desk for preparing *animation* artwork. Also: Device for viewing photographic *transparencies*.

light bridge: walkway over *grid*. Called *gantry* in Britain.

light grid: metal girders or lattice suspending lights over *set*.

lighting: controlled illumination. Compare: *natural light*.

lighting cameraman: in Britain, chief camera technician who determines a *shot's* visual components.

light level: illumination intensity, measured in *candelas*.

light meter—exposure meter: *photoelectric cell* device in various formats, measuring direct or reflected illumination intensity in *candelas*.

lightning stick: hand-operated *arc* light producing bright flashes.

light plot: *luminaire* placement plan. Compare: *floor plan, prop plot*.

light-struck: film *footage* inadvertently ruined by *exposure* to light. Called *edge-fogged* in Britain.

light valve: *photoelectric cell* converting electrical *signals* into fluctuations of a beam of light, and vice versa. See: *sound head*.

lily: standard color swatch test chart for precise *film printing* control; similar to television's *color bars*. Compare: *china girl*.

limbo: photographic background with no visual frame of reference. See: *no-seam, cyc*. Compare: *set*.

limited animation: *frame*-at-a-time cinematography of two-dimensional material with slightly-altering subject and/or camera movement. *Projection* at *speed* (24 *fps*) gives illusion of actual motion. See: *animation*. Compare: *stop motion*.

limiting resolution: discriminatable number of *test pattern* horizontal lines.

limpet—sucker: in Britain, rubber suction cup temporarily attaching equipment to any smooth surface.

line: individual electron beam *sweep* across *camera target* or *picture tube* (in 52.3 *microseconds*); in the U.S., 525 such *sweeps* to each *frame*—in Britain, 625. See: *blanking interval*. *Also:* Material in *transmission*. See: *line check*. Also: Imaginary *tape/film* camera position boundary. See: *crossing the line*.

line amplifier: *amplifier feeding transmission circuit*.

linebeat—meshbeat: annoying moiré effect caused by certain aberrant linear characteristics of *image orthicon pickup tubes* and color television *picture tubes*. Also caused by horizontal subject patterns.

line check: off-the-*line* copy of *air* material prior to *transmission*. Compare: *air check*.

line cord—power cord: electric supply wires.

line feed: *remote signal* transmitted by *cable* (usually telephone company-leased).

line frequency: number of horizontal television *frame scans* per second; nominally more than 15,000.

line monitor: *control room monitor* showing *on-air* material. Compare: *preview*.

line-of-sight: high-band *transmission* (such as *television* and *FM*) to *receivers* lying between *transmitting antenna* and horizon.

line test: in Britain, rough initial *animation* execution, photographed to check movement.

line up: adjust proper relationship of any elements: *soundtracks,* camera *signals,* etc. Also: 1,000-*Hz audio signal*.

lineup: *broadcast stations scheduling* a *network feed*.

linkman: in Britain, *documentary*/news presenter or *compere*.

lippy: in Britain, lipstick.

lip sync(hronization): simultaneous *recording* and photography of an *on-camera* speaker (or other sound source); crucial during facial *close-up*. Lip sync can also be added after *silent* photography by *dubbing* against picture. Also: Mouthing words to *pre-recorded audio* (such as a song). Compare: *wild track.*

liquid gate—wet gate: *printing* process placing tetrachlorethylene coating solution on *negative film* to minimize any surface defects.

lissajous pattern: visual *oscilloscope* comparison of *frequency* and sine wave.

live: *broadcast* of something actually happening; not a *recording.* Also: In active use. Also: With *acoustical reverberation.* Compare: *dead.*

live action: normal *motion picture* camera photography.

live announcer: announcer, usually local, adding a *tag* to *recorded commercial* message.

live fade: performer moving *off mike* while speaking. Compare: *board fade.*

live-on-tape: television *program recorded* to length in *real time* without pause or later *editing.*

live tag: local *commercial* information (retail store name, price, etc.) at the end of *recorded broadcast* advertisement.

LLTV—low-light television: *closed-circuit* systems operating below 0.5 *lumens*/ft^2.

load: equipment power consumption. Also: Fill *camera magazine* with *film; recorder* with *tape.*

load in: bring production materials onto *set.* Compare: *strike.*

local: *programming*/advertising generated within *broadcast station's coverage* area. Compare: *network.*

local advertiser: single-market *client,* usually retail establishment.

local I.D.: local "tag" sponsorship at tail of national *commercial.*

location: non-*studio* photographic site, usually a *background* not otherwise available.

location fee: payment for use of *location* and its facilities. Called *facilities fee* in Britain.

location scouting—survey: *pre-production* assessment of proposed *remote* broadcast site. Called *recce* or *reccy* in Britain (for *reconnaissance*).

locked off: see *tied off.*

log: *FCC*-required record of *program*, technical and maintenance record of *station's* daily *broadcast* performance. Compare: *affidavit*.

logo—logotype: concise graphic design usually incorporating manufacturer's name.

long: *program* material running beyond allotted time. Compare: *short*.

long lens: optical system making distant objects appear near. Called *long focus* in Britain. See: *telephoto*. Compare: *diopter lens*.

long-playing—33⅓ rpm: standard *phonograph disk* rotation speed. Compare: *extended play*.

long skip: *transmission signal* multi-reflection (up to 8,000 miles). See: *skip effect*. Compare: *short skip*.

long wave—radio wave: *electromagnetic radiation* over 60 meters long, traveling in space at speed of light. See: *short wave*.

loop: length of *film* (or *tape*) *spliced head*-to-*tail* for continuous *projection* (or *playback*). Also: Purposely slack section of *film* between *projector* picture *gate* and *sound head*, absorbing shock of intermittent *claw* movement. See: *pullup*. Also: Circular *cable network*.

looping: *recording lip-synchronized* dialogue against existing *film* picture (and often over existing *sound*). (Called *dubbing* on East Coast.) Also: *Coax* termination *circuitry* minimizing *signal distortion*.

loose: camera subject *framing* with considerable top and side room. Compare: *tight*.

LOP—least objectionable program: theory regarding television *viewing* as default rather than design activity.

lose the light: *control room* switch to another camera (indicated by *tally light*). Also: Have *exterior shooting* halted by darkness.

lose the loop: accidentally shorten the purposely slack section of *film* between *projector* picture *gate* and *sound head*, resulting in loss of *synchronization*. See: *pullup*.

loss: reduction in *signal* strength *level* during *distribution*, usually expressed in *db*.

lot: large outdoor *studio* area used for *set* construction and *filming*. See: *ext.* Compare: *sound stage.*

loudness: subjective measure of *audio playback intensity* that also includes *high* and *low frequency equalization.* See: *Fletcher-Munson effect, volume.*

loudspeaker—speaker: device *transducing* electronic *signals* into audible *sound waves.* See: *tweeter, woofer.*

low band: original *video tape recording* technique utilizing the 5.5 to 6.5 *megahertz band* (with considerable *signal-to-noise ratio*); or, equipment for such *recording.* (Note: *HIGH-band video tapes* cannot be *played back* on *low-band* equipment.)

low boy: very low *high hat* camera *mount.*

low contrast filter: *lens* filter to mute colors, soften shadows.

low frequency distortion: television *distortion* below 15.75 *kHz.*

low gain—low level: *signal level* of one *millivolt* or less.

low key: dim illumination emphasizing lower *gray scale* and producing few or no bright areas. Compare: *high key.*

lows—low frequencies: audible sound *frequencies* starting around 50 *hertz.* Compare: *highs, middle range.*

low Z: see *Z.*

LP: "long-playing" 33⅓ *rpm phonograph disk.*

LS—long shot: tiny performer(s) against vast *background.* Compare: *FS.*

LSI—large-scale integration: more than 100 miniaturized *circuits* on a three-inch wafer. Compare: *SSI.*

LUF: lowest usable *frequency* not absorbed in *ionosphere.*

lumen—LM: one *candela* (0.98 *foot candles*) of light covering a square foot of surface. See: *footlambert.*

lumens per watt—LPW—efficacy: number of *lumens* produced by light source for each *watt* of power applied.

luminaire: combination of support, *housing, lens, lamp* (*bulb*) and power *connector* of a light-producing device.

luminance: measure of light (formerly called *brightness*) leaving a surface in a particular direction, measured in *footlamberts* on a *gray scale.*

luminance signal: *NTSC* color "brightness" *signal;* the *chrominance signal* supplies the *hue* and *saturation.*

luminescence—fluorescence: production of light (and heat) by energy absorption. Compare: *phosphorescence*.

lux: (metric measurement) one *lumen* per square meter of surface; 10 *lux* equal approximately one *foot candle*. See: *candela*.

LVR—longitudinal video recording: lateral (not *quad, helical*) *video tape recording* technique; one 2-hour configuration utilizes 48 parallel bands of *video/audio signal* at 160 *i.p.s.*, reversing direction (in $^1/_{10}$ sec.) along an 8mm *video tape*.

LWT—London Weekend: one of British *IBA*'s *"Big Five"* (the *Central Companies*).

M

Ma Bell: Bell System telephone companies linked through American Telephone & Telegraph Company (*A.T. & T.*).

macbeth: glass *filter* converting *tungsten* or *quartz* light source to daylight *color balance*. Also: *Fluorescent* viewer lamp with that characteristic.

macky: in Britain, makeup.

macrolens: *close-up* camera *lens*.

Madison Avenue: location of several major New York advertising *agencies*.

magazine: lightproof container feeding *loaded film raw stock* through a *motion picture* camera and taking it up after *exposure;* usually 400 or 1,000-foot capacity.

magenta: purplish-red subtractive element of color *negative film;* complementary of (producing) green. See: *cyan, yellow.*

Magicam: computerized two-camera *chromakey* process utilizing miniaturized *sets.* Compare: *minicam, Steadicam.*

magnetic head: one of three magnetic *gaps* (*erase head, record head, playback head*) in contact with *tape* in *audio recording.* Also: *Record* (also *playback*) *head*(s) in *video tape recording.*

magnetic recording: (from principles developed by Poulsen in 1898) *video* and/or *audio recording* effected by changing polarity of microscopic particles of metallic *oxide* (on *film* or *tape base*) by passing them across modulated *magnetic* field *gap*.

mag(netic) stripe: clear *35mm sprocketed film* with continuous metallic *oxide* strip for *recording* a single (or mixed) *soundtrack*. Called *zonal stripe* in Britain. Compare: *full coat*.

magnetic track: magnetic oxide *soundtrack* on *composite film base* (replacing *optical track*). Compare: *mag track*.

Magnetophon: original (German) magnetic *tape recorder*.

magnetostatic: field produced by stationary magnet. Compare: *electrostatic*.

mag track: loosely, a magnetically *recorded soundtrack;* usually on a *16mm* or *35mm film* base. Compare: *magnetic track*.

mains: in Britain, electric power supply line.

main title: major information on *program* content, at or near beginning of a *telecast*. Compare: *credits, subtitle, title*.

major sponsor: advertiser with most *commercials* in multiple-sponsor program. See: *alternate sponsorship*.

makegood: free *station re-run* of poorly *transmitted* or omitted *commercial*.

makeup: performer's facial "paint 'n' powder," to balance lighting and camera requirements.

makeup artist: union craftsman applying the above.

male: *connector* insert. Compare: *female*.

mandated: in Britain, *program* whose *transmission* is required of all *IBA* companies.

mandatory: disclaimer or other legally required information in body of a *commercial,* usually *video* (in barely legible type). See: *title*.

M & E—music and (sound) effects: *film soundtracks* (separate or combined) of non-dialogue *audio* elements, essential for foreign-language *dubbing,* etc.

Marconi: Italian engineer pioneering *radio signal transmission* (1895).

Marechal: proprietary French power-cable *connection* system.

mark: small piece of tape placed on *studio* floor, accurately repositioning *scenery* or performer. See: *hit the mark, miss the mark*.

marketing: all aspects of product distribution and sales.

"mark it"—"sticks": cameraman's call for *synchronizing clapstick* action.

married: in Britain, *composite* (*picture* with *optical soundtrack*) *film print*.

mask: modified rectangular frame with rounded corners, covering television *picture tube* edges. Also: Interchangeable metal cutout to vary size of *film projection gate*. Also: Opaque shape to screen a *set* light. See: *flag, gobo*. Compare: *cutter, dot, finger*.

masking: partially covering one sound with another.

mass erase—bulk erase: magnetic-field device to *degauss* all *recording tape* on a *reel* without unspooling. Compare: *erase head*.

master: original completed *video tape recording*. Compare: *dub, dupe*. Also: Original *cut phonograph* or *video disk* (or its molds). Also: Single *antenna* serving multiple *receivers*.

master control: *broadcast* facility control center. Called *CCR* (central control room) in Britain. Also: Control panel group *fader*.

mastering: *cutting* original *phonograph* or *video disk* and molding it for reproduction.

master shot: complete *scene* sequence. See: *establishing shot*.

master/slave(s): *re-recording* system playing back *original tape* into *dubbing recorder(s)*. Compare: *AC transfer, bifilar, dynamic duplication*.

match cut: *editing* to another camera position at the identical moment of an action. Compare: *jump cut*.

match dissolve: *opticaling* to an identical camera position.

matching—negative cutting: matching *film negative* material to *edited work print*. See: *pull negative*. Also: **matching:** *impedance alignment*.

matrix: *quadruphonic FM broadcast* and *recording/playback* system, encoding two extra *channels* atop two existing *stereo channels*. See: *SQ, QS*. Compare: *discrete*.

Matrix H: *BBC* compatible (*mono/stereo*) *quadruphonic broadcast* system.

·117·

Matsushita: major Japanese electronic manufacturer.

matte—matteing: optical or electronic insertion of an image into a selected background. See: *chromakey.* Compare: *rotoscope.* Also: **matte:** dull or diffuse, compared to mirror-like.

matte box: squarish *lens hood* device used for sunshade and wide variety of in-the-camera *optical effects.*

matteing amplifier: television *special effects generator (SEG).*

matteing out: *optically* eliminating an element in the *film frame.*

matte ride: undesirable outlines around *matted* element. See: *ringing.*

MATV—master antenna television system: *antenna* arrangement serving concentration of television *receivers.* Compare: *CATV.*

Mayflower Doctrine: 1941 *FCC* decision (reversed eight years later) proscribing broadcast "editorializing."

MC—master of ceremonies: show host. Called *compere* in Britain. Compare: *announcer, narrator.* Also: **MC:** *megacycle.*

MCU—medium close-up: performers waist-up. Called *close shot* (*CS*) in Britain. Compare: *MS, CU.*

MDS—multi-point distribution service: *pay cable* interconnection.

media (department): *advertising agency* division charged with recommending *client* purchase of *broadcast time* periods. See: *campaign, schedule, time buyer.*

media market: geographic area defined by *coverage* pattern of a market's media (usually television).

medium: means of communicating an advertising message.

medium wave: *amplitude modulation radio broadcasting.*

megabit: one-millionth *bit.*

megacycle—MC: *frequency* unit equal to 1 million *cycles per second;* now called *megahertz (MHz).*

megahertz—MH—MHz: (see above; renamed after discoverer of electromagnetic or *radio* waves) one million *hertz. FM radio* operates from 88 to 108 *MHz.*

megawatt—MW: one million *watts;* 1,000 *kW.*

memory: electronic information *retrieval* system. Specifically, *semiconductor chip* storing *bit* information.

meshbeat—linebeat: annoying moiré effect caused by certain aberrant linear characteristics of *image orthicon pickup tubes* and color television *picture tubes*. Also caused by horizontal subject patterns.

metal halide—MH: *AC*-only mercury arc lamp.

meter: television audience research device installed in "sample homes" to record *program* preferences. See: *Audimeter, SIA*. Also: See *v. i. meter*.

metro: standard metropolitan statistical area as defined by U.S. Office of Management and Budget; contiguous counties containing at least one city with 50,000 population.

Mev: 1 million electron-*volts*. Compare: *Gev*.

mho: (*ohm* spelled backwards) measurement of admittance (reciprocal of *impedance*).

microgroove: narrow V-shaped track (approximately 200 per inch) on *long-playing* or *extended play phonograph disk*.

micron: one-millionth of a meter; roughly $1/25$ *mil*. Equal to 10,000 *ångströms*.

microphone—mike—mic: device *transducing sound waves* into electrical impulses. See: *cardioid, ceramic, condenser, crystal, dynamic, eightball, lavalier, ribbon, rifle*.

microphone: *audio frequency* equipment noise caused by mechanical shock or vibration.

microprocessor: tiny *semi-conductor chip* containing more than 5,000 *transistors*. See: *integrated circuit*.

microsecond: one-millionth second.

microwave: line-of-sight (usually five miles or more) cable-less system relaying *broadcast signals* on *wavelengths* of less than one meter. First used by Pope Pius XII (15 miles in 1933). U.S. transcontinental *relay* installed 1951. Compare: *coaxial cable, satellite*.

mid-bass: standard *audio frequency* range (60–240 *Hz*). Compare: *bass, mid-range, mid-treble, treble*.

mid-range: standard *audio frequency* range (240–1,000 *Hz*). Compare: *bass, mid-bass, mid-treble, treble*.

mid-treble: standard *audio frequency* range (1,000–3,500 *Hz*). Compare: *bass, mid-bass, mid-range, treble*.

midshot: in Britain, performer's whole body in *frame*.

mil: one-thousandth inch.

milk sweep: small J-shaped translucent white *scenery* piece, eliminating any visual frame of reference. See: *limbo*. Compare: *cyc, no-seam*.

millimicron: one twenty-five-millionth inch.

millisecond: one-thousandth second.

millivolt: one-thousandth *volt*.

mini-brute—nine light: nine grouped 650*w* *tungsten-halogen* bulbs.

minicam: *hand-held ENG* camera. Compare: *Magicam, Steadicam*.

minimum focus: shortest distance at which a *lens* is focusable.

minute: *60-second commercial* message; in television *film,* offering 58 seconds of *audio*. Compare: *thirty, twenty, ten*.

mired—micro reciprocal degree: 1,000,000 divided by appropriate *Kelvin* value, for a more workable *color temperature* rating. See: *decamired*.

mirror ball: reflecting globe covered with tiny mirrored chips; essential to dance marathon ballroom photography.

mirror shot: doubling *shot* depth by pointing camera at large mirror. Also useful for overhead *POV*s.

mirror shutter: *reflex shutter* system enabling camera operator to view *shot* in progress. Compare: *beam splitter, intermittent shutter*.

miss the mark: move to a pre-determined *set* point—and miss. Compare: *hit the mark*.

Mitchell: workhorse American *35mm* camera. Most common model is (non-*reflex*) *BNC*.

Mitsubishi: major Japanese electronics manufacturer.

mix: session in *re-recording studio*. See: *audio mix*. Also: To *dissolve*. Also: Optimized media selection.

mixed feed: television camera scene lineup technique; one camera's *output* is fed into another's *viewfinder*.

mixer: engineer handling *mix* control *console*. Called *recordist* in Britain. Also: The *audio* or *video mixing console* itself.

mixing studio: recording facility equipped to electronically combine two or more *audio* elements into a single final *sound-*

track, usually against picture *projection.* Compare: *worldize.*

mm—millimeter: one-thousandth meter.

MNA—multi-network area: Nielsen's group of 30 major markets where programs of all three *networks* can be received over local television *stations.*

mobile unit: vehicle or equipment used for *recording* or *transmitting* television *signals* from a location.

mob scene: group of actors acting as a crowd.

mockup: imitative section of a large scenic *prop,* built to scale rather than in miniature.

mode: electronic setting activating specific *circuit(s).*

modeling—counter key: illumination directly opposite to *key light.*

model sheet: *animation* cartoon drawings showing character in various poses. See: *animation designer.*

modulate: vary the amplitude, *frequency* or *phase* of *carrier* wave with a *signal.* Compare: *unmodulated.*

modulation: *recorded audio signal* patterns; called *mods* in Britain.

module: interchangeable electronic component.

moiré: undesirable optical effect caused by one set of closely spaced lines improperly imposed over another. In television, *picture* disturbance caused by interference beats of similar *frequencies.*

Molevator: 6–14 ft. high power-operated extensible stand for *brutes* and other large *spotlights.*

Molniya: USSR *satellites* (I, II, etc.) in *Orbita* transmission system; some non-*geosynchronous* to cover Soviet polar areas.

monaural: single sound source intended for both ears. Compare: *binaural.*

monitor: television *receiver* (often without *channel* selector or audio components) connected to transmission source by wire. Also: To check *recording* in progress.

monochromatic: tones or gradations of a single color or *hue.*

monochrome: black, grays and white.

monochrome transmission: *signal* wave representing *brightness* components of a television picture but not its color (*chrominance*) values.

monophonic: single-channel ¼″ *audio tape recording, full* or *half-track*.

monopod: single-leg camera support.

montage: visual blending of several *scenes*. Also: In Europe, the *film editing* process (from Fr. *monter* = to set up).

MOR—middle-of-road: *radio station format* featuring non-rock music, news, weather, sports, etc.

Morse code: "dot-dash" *radiotelegraphy* (with letter symbols developed 1838 by telegraph inventor).

MOS: *silent film shot* (mythically requested by 1930's refugee Hollywood director: "*mit-o*ut *s*prache!"). Also: Metal oxide *semi-conductor*.

mosaic—target: camera *pickup tube* storage surface (over 350,000 *photosensitive* dots) *scanned* by *electron beam*.

motion picture: connected series of *still* images presenting illusion of movement *projected* on *screen* (or television *tube* face).

mount: camera *lens* or *luminaire* socket.

Moviola: horizontal/vertical *film*-and-*sound editing* machines. See: *Kem, Steenbeck*.

MPA: multiple product television *commercial*.

mps: miles per second.

MRA—metro rating area: *ARB* audience research classification of U.S. metropolitan markets.

MS—medium shot: performer's whole body in *frame*. Also called *midshot* in Britain. Compare: *FS, MCU*.

MSO: *multiple* (*CATV*) systems operator.

muddy: indistinct.

mug: overreact facially.

multi-camera: simultaneous *filming/taping* from two or more camera positions.

multipath: reflected departure(s) from direct *broadcast signal* path. See: *ghost*.

multiplane: layered *cel animation* technique.

multiple interference: cancelled sound *frequencies* from two *microphones* in close proximity.

multiple image: *frame* composed of several different picture sources.

multiplex: single *conductor* (or equipment) accepting/*transmitting* two or more simultaneous *signals* (or *feeds*). Compare: *duplex, simplex*.

multiplexer: mirror or prism device feeding *images* from several *projection* sources into television *station's camera chain*.

mute: in Britain, *silent film*.

Mutoscope: early *motion picture* "peepshow" viewer (Casler, 1894).

N

NA(RT)B—National Association of (Radio & Television) Broadcasters: standard-setting *broadcast station* membership organization. Compare: *AA, AAAA, Advertising Council, ANA, IPA, ISBA.*

NAB Code: minimum *programming* and advertising standards for *NARTB* member *stations: radio*—18 *commercial* minutes per hour; television—16 *commercial* minutes per hour. Compare: *CAP.*

NAB curve: *audio playback equalization* standard.

NABET—National Association of Broadcast Employees and Technicians: *broadcast* technicians' union.

nadgers: in Britain, equipment trouble.

NAEB—National Association of Educational Broadcasters: *station* operators' membership organization.

naff—US: in Britain, useless, no good. Compare: *NG.*

Nagra: high-quality portable ¼" *audio tape recorder* for *location production.*

nanosecond: one-billionth (i.e., one-thousand-millionth) second.

NARB—National Advertising Review Board: self-regulatory industry group.

narrator: ''neutral'' *on-* or *off-camera* performer telling *program* story. Called *commentator* in Britain. Compare: *announcer, MC.*

narrowcast: public *signal transmission* by any other mass medium than *broadcast*.

narrow-gauge—substandard: *film* less than *35mm* wide.

NASA—National Aeronautics and Space Administration: government agency administering communications *satellite* program. See: *ATS-6*.

national: higher rate charged more-than-one-market advertisers by stations also offering *local retail rate*.

National ARBitron: audience survey technique utilizing mailed-in listening *diaries*. See: *ARB*. Compare: *Pulse*.

NATTKE—National Association of Theatrical, Television and Kine Employees: in Britain, trade union representing studio carpenters. *prop* men, *grips, projectionists, wardrobe, makeup,* etc.

natural light: daylight. Compare: *lighting*

NBC—National Broadcasting Company: U.S. *broadcasting network,* owned by conglomerate *RCA Corporation*. See: *Thirty Rock*.

NCTA—National Cable Television Association: *cable* system operators' membership organization.

needle: *meter* dial indicator. Also: *Stylus* element of *phonograph* arm, *tracking record grooves*.

needle drop: single use of *licensed stock music* composition.

needletime: in Britain, *broadcasting recorded* music.

negative: *film* image or television *signal* with opposite tonal (and color) values to original subject material. Also: Lower electrical *potential*. Compare: *positive*.

negative cutting—pulling: matching *film negative* material to *edited work print*.

nemo: early acronymically-derived telephone company designation: "*n*ot *e*manating *m*ain *o*ffice." Now any *remote* broadcast *signal* origination point. See: *pickup*.

net: metal or gauze *spotlight diffuser;* also called *lavender* in Britain. Also: A *network*.

NET—National Educational Television: educational television *programming* organization. See: *ETV, CPB, PBS*.

net rating points—NRP: total number of *rating points* for specific television advertising *schedule,* eliminating *duplicated* viewing. Compare: *gross rating points.*

net weekly circulation: audience survey estimate of unduplicated *households* viewing a television *station* for at least five consecutive minutes at least once during the week.

network—net: one of three huge entertainment/news combines (*ABC, CBS, NBC*) supplying *programming* and advertising material to *affiliated* U.S. *broadcast stations.* Initial network experimentation (*radio*) via telephone lines (1922). Compare: *independent, local.* Also: *Stations* interconnected for *broadcast* of same material.

network feed: New York-, Chicago- or Los Angeles-originated *program,* fed to *stations* across the U.S. via *AT&T cables* and *microwave* links. Compare: *bicycling, DB.*

networking: assembling a program/station lineup.

neutral density filter—ND: *lens filter* reducing transmitted light without affecting its color, *contrast* or *definition.* Used on excessively illuminated subjects.

news block: extended news *programming.*

newscaster: reader/presenter of news items. Compare: *anchorman, commentator.*

NG: no good!

nickel-cadmium—NiCad: portable heavy-duty rechargeable *storage battery.* See: *power pack.*

(A.C.) Nielsen: television audience survey service employing *Audimeter* devices to record *viewing* habits in 1,200 sample U.S. homes. Issues *NTI* (Nielsen Television Index) bi-weekly audience measurements. See: *SIA.* Compare: *ARB.*

nighttime: broadcast *time* period from 7:00 P.M. to 11:00 P.M. (or midnight).

nine light—mini-brute: nine grouped 650*w tungsten-halogen lamps.*

nitrate: see *base.*

nixie: computer light indicating electronic information.

nod shot: in Britain, *film* or *video tape* shot of interviewer; avoids *jump-cut editing* of interviewee.

no fax: rehearsal without technical *facilities.*

noise: random energy generated by *voltages* within an electronic device, creating extraneous *sound* or *picture signal interference*. Compare: *snow*.

noise bar: picture *breakup* on *helical scan video tape playback,* usually during *still framing*.

non-air commercial: *broadcast* advertising message specially prepared (at lower *talent* fees) for various non-*broadcast* audience research techniques. See: *black box*.

non-commercial: *broadcasting* without advertising support; 11% of all radio (lowest 20 *FM* channels), 35% of all television *stations* (1978).

non-compatibility: inability of one system to *retrieve* information stored by another. Compare: *compatibility, interface*.

non-composite: *video signal* lacking *synchronization* information. Compare: *composite*.

non-directional: *microphone* with uniform areas of sensitivity. Compare: *directional*.

non-duplication: *FCC* prohibition on identical *programming* by twin *AM/FM* facilities.

non-segmented—single-scan: *"Type C"* 1" *video tape* format (*Ampex, Sony*) *recording* one complete television *field* during each *head* pass; permits *freeze-framing*. Compare: *segmented*.

northlight: *luminaire* using four indirect 1K *quartz-iodine lamps* for *diffused fill* illumination.

no-seam: very wide paper background in various colors, pulled from large rolls to provide no visual frame of photographic reference. See: *limbo*. Compare: *cyc, milk sweep*.

notch: shallow *cue* cut in edge of *film negative* for *print timing* purposes. Compare: *tab*. Also: Film *emulsion* edge marks for *darkroom* identification. Also: Electronic *filter* rejecting narrow *band* of *frequencies*.

NPACT—National Public Affairs Center for Television: Washington-based *PBS*-controlled television *program production* unit.

NPR—National Public Radio: *CPB*-financed *live/tape* affiliation of more than 150 full-service *non-commercial stations* (established 1970).

·127·

NQRC—National Quadruphonic Radio Committee: *discrete*-oriented industry-sponsored group.

NSRC—National Stereophonic Radio Committee: *radio* engineering group established 1959 to recommend *FM stereo broadcast* standards to *FCC*.

NTAs—Nielsen Television Areas: standard U.S. market areas established by *Nielsen* survey service.

NTI—Nielsen Television Index Rating: bi-weekly *network* television show audience size (only) *rating* report, based on *Audimeter* records from 1,200 *households;* the industry standard for national network audience estimates, available a few weeks after each *telecast*. See: *SIA*.

NTSC—National Television System Committee: *broadcast* engineering group established by U.S. television industry in early 1940's to recommend *b/w transmission* standards *(525-line,* 60 *field)* to the *FCC*. Reactivated in early 1950's to recommend color *transmission* standards; unlike newer *PAL* and *SECAM* systems, NTSC color *phase* relationships are easily *distorted* (occasionally identified as *"n*ever *t*wice the *s*ame *c*olor").

NUJ: in Britain, National Union of Journalists.

null: *dead microphone* area.

number board: in Britain, several *frames* of a small blackboard with full *scene* information, photographed at the head of each *take;* often a hinged *clapstick* provides visual/sound *synchronization*. Also called *take board*.

O

O & O's: *broadcast stations* owned *and* operated by a *network* (limited by *FCC* ruling to 5 *VHF*-TV, 2 *UHF*-TV and 7 *radio*), usually located in most profitable U.S. markets. Compare: *affiliate, independent.*

OB: in Britain, outside (*remote* location) broadcast. See: *recce.*

OB van: in Britain, self-contained *control room*-and-equipment *broadcast* vehicle, often with *microwave* capability.

OC—on camera: television performer both heard and seen. Compare: *off camera.*

øersted: unit of *tape recording* magnetic field strength. See: *coercivity.*

OF: optical fibers. See: *fiber optics.*

off camera—VO—voice over: television performer heard but not seen. Called *commentary over, out-of-vision, OOV* in Britain. Compare: *OC.*

off-line: (less expensive) use of non-standard *production* equipment. Compare: *on-line.*

off mike: speech directed away from the *microphone*, simulating distant sound. Compare: *on mike.*

offset: sound overlap from previous or following *scene.*

offstage: anywhere outside camera view. Compare: *onstage.*

ohm—O: basic unit of electrical *resistance.* Compare: *ampere, mho, volt, watt.*

Ohm's Law: (1827) *voltage* (E) = *amperage*(I) × *resistance* (R).

OIRT—International Radio and Television Organization: world telecommunications standards group.

olivette: obsolete *floodlight*.

omega wrap: *video tape* wind configuration around *helical scan drum*. Compare: *alpha wrap*.

omnidirectional: *microphone* with circular *pickup* pattern.

omnies: non-identifiable crowd *extras,* or their murmuring voices. Called *rhubarb* in Britain. See: *crowd noise, walla-walla*.

on-air: *program* being *broadcast* or *recorded*.

1.5 head system: *SONY helical video tape* design utilizing separate *head* for *vertical interval signals*.

one light: *positive film print* made without *intensity* and/or *color correction* for initial *editorial* work. See: *dailies, rushes*.

one shot: single performance not scheduled for re-*broadcast*. See: *special*. Compare: *across the board, strip*.

one-step: *phonograph disk duplication* method, using a backed silverplating of original *acetate recording* for low-quantity vinyl *pressings*. Compare: *two-step*.

1,000-hertz tone: standard *audio* reference tone *signal*. See: *beep*(*s*).

on-line: use of standard *production* equipment. Compare: *off-line*.

on mike: speaking directly into *microphone*. Compare: *off mike*.

on ones (two, threes, etc.): *animation* photography of identical *cel* once, twice, three times, etc.

onstage: within camera view. Compare: *offstage*.

on the air: *broadcasting*.

on the fly: choosing *video edit* point while *tape* is moving.

on the nose: to exact time.

OOP: out-of-pocket (expense).

OOT: out of town.

opaque: not transmitting light.

opaquer: *animation* artist applying paint to inked backs of *cels*.

open call: non-restricted *audition*.

open door: in Britain, minority viewpoint *programming* over standard *broadcasting facilities*.

open end: *program* with no specific scheduled completion time.

Also: *Commercial* with space and time for added local material.

open mike: live *microphone*.

open reel—reel-to-reel: *tape transport* system with separated supply (*feed*) and *take-up reels*. Compare: *cartridge, cassette*.

open up: enlarge camera *lens aperture*.

operations department: *broadcast station scheduling* group.

operations sheet: daily *station broadcast schedule*.

operator: in Britain, technician actually operating (and usually loading) the camera.

optical effects—opticals: artificial visual *effects: fades, dissolves, wipes, superimpositions,* and similar *transitional* devices.

optical fibers: see *fiber optics*.

optical glass: high-quality *lens* material.

optical house: facility for processing final *film negative* to include selected *optical effects* and *titling*.

optical negative: final *printing negative* (picture). Compare: *optical track*.

optical printer: *optical house printing* machine producing final *optical negative:* "Film cameras take pictures; optical printers complete them."

optical track: final *soundtrack printing negative*. Compare: *optical negative*. Also: Composite *film's* patterned photographic strip converted into *sound* by *exciter lamp* and *photoelectric cell*. See: *variable area, variable density*. Compare: *magnetic track*.

optical transfer: duplication of fully-*mixed audio tape track* into a *negative film soundtrack*.

optical view finder: device permitting operator to see and frame picture the camera is taking.

optional cut: predetermined deletion.

ORACLE—Optional Reception of Announcements by Coded Line Electronics: British (*IBA*) system for *digital transmission* of printed information, utilizing television *signal blanking intervals* at seven *megabits* per second. See: *Ceefax*. Compare: *ANTIOPE, SLICE, Teletext, Viewdata*.

Orbita: USSR domestic *satellite transmission* system, utilizing *Molniya satellites.*

original: initial camera *negative* (or *video tape recording*) before *post production.*

origination: U.S. *network feed* point, usually New York, Chicago or Los Angeles.

ORTF—Office de Radiodiffusion-Télévision Française: French state-controlled *broadcasting network,* dismembered in 1974 into seven separate entities. Compare: *BBC, FCC, RAI.* See: *SFP.*

orthicon: see *image orthicon.*

Oscar: Academy (of Motion Picture Arts and Sciences) Award statuette. Also: In Britain, adjustable quartered *luminaire diffuser.* Also: *O*rbital *S*atellite *C*arrying *A*mateur *R*adio; first (of seven) launched December 12, 1961.

oscillator: electronic device producing specific *frequencies.*

oscilloscope—scope: *cathode-ray tube* device for visual electronic *signal* analysis.

OT—Office of Telecommunications: U.S. Department of Commerce unit.

OTO: *commercial* scheduled one time only.

OTP—Office of Telecommunications Policy: controversial White House *broadcasting* policy pipeline.

out: movement from. Compare: *in.*

outage: electric power failure.

out-cue: closing words of *cue* line. Compare: *in-cue.*

outgrade: eliminate a *commercial player* in *editing.* Compare: *downgrade.*

outlet: female *connector* (usually for *power*).

outline: brief written summary of proposed *program* idea.

out of focus: distorted or fuzzy picture.

out of frame: not in camera view. Also: Faulty *projection* of portions of two *frames* at once. Called *out of rack* in Britain.

out of sync: mis*aligned sound* and *picture* elements. Compare: *in sync.* Also: Absence of *synchronization* between television *receiver* and *transmitted signal,* causing vertical *roll* or horizontal displacement.

·132·

out of vision—OOV—commentary over: in Britain, performer heard but not seen.

output: useful *power* or *signal* from piece of electronic equipment. Also: Equipment *power* or *signal* transfer *terminal*. Compare: *input*.

outtake: *taped* or *filmed scene* discarded in final *edit*. Compare: *selected take*.

overcrank: operate *motion picture* camera at faster-than-normal *frame speed*, producing "slow-motion" effect in normal *projection*. Called *turn fast* in Britain. Compare: *undercrank*.

overexpose: too-slow *shutter speed* and/or overwide *aperture* matched to *film emulsion* characteristics, resulting in undesirable "dark" *negative* (or *reversal*) and "light" *print*. Compare: *underexpose*.

overload: input of power or *signal* beyond equipment's capability to distribute or reproduce, causing *distortion* or failure.

overmodulation: *audio overload*.

overscale: *talent* fee in excess of union minimums.

overscan: television *picture* area beyond normal *receiver mask*.

oxide: microscopic oxidized metallic particles (usually about 400 millionths of an inch thick) coated onto a *base* to form *magnetic tape* or *film track*.

P

P: indication to *film laboratory* to *print* specific *take*.

PA—public address system: public local *microphone/loudspeaker* system. Compare: *PL, talkback*.

package: completely prepared *program* or series offered for sale. See: *syndication*.

package plan: *broadcast station's* specially priced *spot time* combination sale offer, usually on weekly or monthly basis.

packager: company producing a *program package*.

packing density: amount of magnetic information potentially *recordable* in a given space.

pack shot: in Britain, product *close-up*.

pad: *program* material to fill time. Compare: *bumper, cushion*.

paint pots: *console* color control *rheostats*.

pairing: *interlace* failure where alternate *scan lines* fall on top of or very near one another.

PAL—phase alternate line: British, Western European, Scandinavian, Australian (1975), and South African (1976) color transmission standard (*625-line, 50-*field) developed by Bruch; technically more complex (requiring millionth second accuracy) than U.S. *NTSC* system and less subject to color *distortion;* the *color burst's subcarrier phase* is inverted with each *scan line,* minimizing *hue* error. Compare: *SECAM*.

Panasonic: major Japanese electronics manufacturer.

Panavision 35: *wide-screen film* process; 2.35:1.

pancake: water-soluble *makeup*. Also: Very low *set* support box. Compare: *apple, riser*.

panchromatic: *b/w film emulsion* sensitive to all colors of visible spectrum.

pan(chromatic) glass: *filter* originally used for *eyeball* evaluation of *monochromatic* values; still useful for calculating sun-vs.-cloud movement, or light path centers.

pan(chromatic) master: positive *b/w finegrain* made from a *color negative,* used to make *b/w dupe negative.*

P&W—pension and welfare: *talent* union retirement benefits, paid by *producer.*

pan handle: handle controlling camera *mount* movement.

pan head: camera *mount* permitting even, controlled *panning.* See: *friction head.*

pan(oramic): camera swivel along horizontal *arc,* from fixed position. Compare: *tilt, track.*

panstick: grease-based *makeup.*

pantograph: overhead *spotlight* suspension mechanism.

papering: in Britain, visual identification—with inserted paper strips—of portions of *film footage.*

parabolic—beam projector—sun spot: *spotlight* projecting narrow, almost parallel light *beam.*

parabolic antenna: *focusable* concave metal or mesh *dish transmitting/receiving* a *line-of-sight signal.*

parabolic (reflector) microphone: concave *dish*-mounted *microphone focusing* distant *sound waves* without distortion.

parallax: angle of divergence between *camera lens* and its *viewfinder.* Can cause *framing* error.

parallels: temporary steel-tube-and-wood high camera platform. Compare: *cherry picker, crane.*

participation: *program* accepting non-competitive spot *commercial insertions.* Compare: *wild spot.*

passive: equipment incapable of power generation or *amplification.*

patch: temporary electronic *circuit connection.*

patch bay—patchboard: see *patch panel.*

patch cord: short *cable* with male *connector jacks* at both ends.

patch panel: temporary *circuit connectors,* often replaced by *switcher.* Called *jackfield* in Britain.

patch plug: *console-*mounted female *cable connection.*

path: *signal* route. Also: *Film/tape* route. See: *lace up.*

pay cable: wired *subscription television* with surcharge for special optional *programming.* See: *premium television, see/fee.* Compare: *pay television, STV.*

payola: sub rosa payment to *broadcast* improperly favorable material, proscribed by Federal Communications Act amendment, 1960. Compare: *freebie, junket, plugola.*

pay television: initiated in New York in 1950, *scrambled* over-the-air *broadcast* television *programming* made available for viewing by coin-operated in-home *decoder.* See *premium television, STV.* Compare: *pay cable, see/fee.*

PBS—Public Broadcasting Service: government-funded "interconnection" distributing national *programming* to over 225 *non-commercial* U.S. television *stations* (occasionally identified as "*p*lenty of *B*ritish *s*hows"). See: *CPB, NET, ETV.*

PD—public domain: creative work not copyrighted or whose copyright restriction has expired. Compare: *license, royalty.*

pea bulb: small *lamp* inside *motion picture* camera, producing *flash frame edit cue.*

peak: maximum *positive* or *negative signal* excursion (excluding *spikes*); *voltage* difference = peak-to-peak.

pedestal—set-up: electronic calibration (interval between *blanking* and *black level pulses*) of television *picture black levels* (*brightness* control on home *receivers*). See: *blacker than black, reference black.* Also: **pedestal:** television camera *dolly* support.

peg bar—peg board—animation board: studded drawing board (or *light box*) accurately aligning sequential *animation cels.*

pencil test: rough *animation* execution, photographed to check movement. Called *line test* in Britain.

penetration: ratio of *HUT's* to total homes, now too high in U.S. to be meaningful statistic.

pentode: *amplifying vacuum tube* with three variably-charged wire mesh *grids* controlling electron flow between *negative filament* (*cathode*) and *positive plate*. Compare: *diode, tetrode, triode*.

perforations: *sprocket* holes. See: *single, double perf.*

permanent set—standing set: *set* in continuing *production* use. Compare: *strike*.

persistence: *phosphor* glow duration following excitation.

persistence of vision: phenomenon of image retention (first enunciated in 1824 by Peter Mark Roget of *Thesaurus* fame) upon which all *film* and television motion illusion is based. Apparently occurs when a succession of static but slightly different images is displayed at greater frequency than either the brain or optic nerve can comprehend (in excess of 10 times per second), creating a kind of visual inertia.

perspective: *audio*-matching the apparent distance of a sound source.

phase: coincidence of *color burst* and reference *signal*.

phase distortion: changes in proper television picture color.

phase modulation: color television *transmission* information (phase shift rate=*frequency;* phase shift degree=*amplitude*).

phasing: standard television camera and *VTR alignment* process.

Phenekistoscope: early slotted-disk *animation* device (Plateau, 1832). Compare: *Praxinoscope, Zöetrope*.

Philips: major European electronics manufacturer.

Phillips screw: standard wood or machine screw with indented "cross" head (requiring Phillips screwdriver). Compare: *Allen screw*.

phon: unit of *loudness,* equal to *decibel* at 1,000 *Hz.*

phonograph: *audio disk* player. Called *gramophone* in Britain. Invented by Edison (or Charles Cros) in 1877.

Phonoscope: 1927 Baird invention recording primitive television *signals* (30 *lines* at 12½ *fps*) on wax *disk*.

phosphors: chemical coatings inside *picture tube,* luminescing when struck by *electron beams*.

phosphorescence: production of light (without heat) through energy absorption. Compare: *fluorescence, luminescence*.

photoconductor: *conductor* permitting variable *current* flow when exposed to light (*photons*). See: *dark current.*

photoelectric cell—photocell: selenium device converting light variations into electrical impulses. See: *exposure meter.*

photoelectric effect: emission of electrons from specific elements when struck by visible light.

photoflood: high-*wattage* (standard light socket) *bulb.*

photography: formation of optical image on sensitized surface by action of light or other radiant energy.

photon: variably-sized discrete bundle of energy in an electromagnetic wave.

photonics: optical-electrical technology.

photoplastic: image-recording technique utilizing light and heat to deform the surface of special plastic film. Compare: *thermoplastic.*

photoresist: material reacting to light by hardening.

photosensitive: reactive to light.

photostat—stat: inexpensively-processed photographic reproduction, usually enlarged or reduced from the original to match available space.

physical edit: mechanical *splice* in *video tape* (obsolete practice).

pickup: *remote broadcast.* Also: *Microphone* sensitivity area. Also: *Phonograph needle* arm (''tone arm''). Also: *Insert* shot. Also: Increase pace of a performance. Also: Television *camera tube* converting optical images into electrical *signals* by an electronic *scanning* process. See: *iconoscope, image isocon, image orthicon, Plumbicon, Saticon, SEC, SIT, vidicon.* Also: **pick up:** move faster.

picosecond: 1/1,000,000,000,000 second.

picture: that portion of the composite television *video signal* above the *blanking signal,* containing the picture information. Also: Loosely, sequential *film frames.*

picture safety: *picture tube* area within which all significant *picture* detail is safely clear of *masks* on even slightly *overscanned receivers.* Compare: *cutoff, lettering safety.*

picture tube: television *receiver* (or *monitor*) *cathode ray* component converting electronic *signal* to fluorescent optical image by *scanning beam intensity* variations. Compare: *camera tube.*

piezoelectric effect: production of electricity from special crystals by mechanical pressure.

pigeons: *monitor noise* in *pulses* or short bursts.

piggyback: *broadcast commercial* combination presenting different products (defined by the *NAB* as ''not related and interwoven'') made by same corporate advertiser. General *station* policy is to charge for a single *time* unit. Compare: *integrated.*

pilot: initial program of proposed *broadcast* series, prepared as demonstration for potential advertising *sponsors.*

pilot pins: see *pins.*

pilots—clip roll—four-framer: in Britain, laboratory *film* test strips of *color balance* ranges prepared to determine final *printing light* selections.

pilot tone: see *sync tone.*

pinch roller—pressure roller—puck: rubber idler wheel holding *recording tape* against *capstan spindle* during *transport.*

pinning: so *overloading audio recording volume* that *v.i. meter needle* bangs against upper pin.

pin rack: sorting bar above editing *bin* for hanging ends of *film* lengths. Called *bin stick* in Britain.

pins: teeth engaging *sprocket* holes centering and pressing each *motion picture film frame* rock-steady in *camera/projector gate.* See: *pressure plate.* Compare: *claw.*

pipe: wire *hookup* for television or *radio program transmission.*

pirate: illegally copy or *broadcast* a *signal.* Also: Tap *CATV transmission* without *subscriber* payment.

pitch: *sound wave frequency.* Also: Distance between two successive *sprocket* holes.

pixels: electronic television *pic*ture *el*ements making up *scan line,* transmitted at the rate of 8½ million per second.

pixlock: adjusted color *synchronization* between two *video tape recorders.*

PL—party line: wired on-*set* communication system. See: *headset.* Compare: *PA, talkback.*

plain lighting: artificial light approximating normal sunlight angles.

plano-convex—PC: simple *lens* with one flat, one convex side. Also: *Spotlight* with such *lens*.

plate: *rewind disk* supporting *film* being wound on *core*. Also: Base *insert* shot. Compare: *external key*. Also: *Positively*-charged *vacuum tube* element.

platen—frame glass: optically clear hinged glass plate holding *cels* flat during *animation* photography.

platter: *phonograph disk*.

playback: *reproduction* of previously-*recorded* material. Also called *playout* in Britain.

players: principal *talent* in a *commercial*. Compare: *extras*.

Players' Guide: oversize directory of performing *talent*. Compare: *Spotlight*.

playlist: *broadcast* musical *recordings*.

playout: in Britain, *reproduction* of previously-*recorded* material.

plop—pip: in Britain, audible *cue* hole or *sync pulse* in *film soundtrack*.

plot: story development. Also: See *light plot, prop plot*.

plug: on-air promotional mention. Also: Mechanical *circuit* inter*connector* (*male*). Compare: *socket*.

plugging box: stage light inter*connector*.

plugola: excessive *on-air* promotion as covert exchange for merchandise. See: *freebie*. Compare: *junket, payola*.

Plumbicon: improved N. V. Phillips color television camera *pickup tube* (30:1 *contrast range*) with *lead oxide target* surface coating, affording a linear *video output*. Also: Camera containing this *tube*. Compare: *image orthicon, vidicon, Saticon*.

pocket: permanent *female* stage light receptacle.

point—rating point: *broadcast* audience size standard. See: *gross rating points, net rating points, share*.

polar curve: graph showing intensity, distribution and emission characteristics of a light source.

polarity: *positive* or *negative* picture characteristics of a *b/w* television *image*. Can be electronically reversed.

polarization: see *circular/horizontal polarization.*

polarized light: light passed through lenses or plates of millions of tiny needle-shaped crystals, blocking all waves except those vibrating in same direction (thus controlling undesirable glare and reflections).

Polaroid filter—pola screen: light-*polarizing lens filter* to reduce glare, reflections or *highlights.*

polecat—jack tube: telescopic wall-braced *luminaire* support.

polyester: *recording tape base* of polyethylene glycol terephthalate.

poop sheet—fact sheet: *copy* points for *announcer's ad-lib* use; opposite of prepared *script.*

pop: contemporary music. Also: Explosive hard consonant (usually "p") in voice *recording.*

pop filter: internal *microphone* device to limit the above. Compare: *windscreen.*

Popoff: Russian *radio* pioneer.

pop-on—pop-off: instantaneously add or subtract new *optical* picture information (usually *titles*) to *frame.* Called *bump-in, bump-out* in Britain. Compare: *fade.*

porch displacement: *level* difference between *front* and *back porch signals.*

porky: in Britain, heavy, exaggerated performance.

portapak (formerly *SONY* trade name): portable (over-the-shoulder) battery-powered miniaturized camera/*recording deck* ensemble. Compare: *backpack.*

position: *commercial* location within a *program* format. Also: Location of *recorded* material on a *tape.* Also: Competitive advertising *copy platform.* See: *purchase proposition.*

positive: *projectible film* with color and/or tonal representation of original subject. Also: Higher electrical *potential.* Compare: *negative.*

positive interlace: exactly-spaced sequential *scanning* of *picture tube field lines.* Compare: *random interlace.*

post dubbing: see *post* production.

post production: any activity after production; generally, *film/tape* completion.

post score: compose/*record* music to existing picture. Compare: *pre-score*.

post sync(hronization): later addition of *synchronous sound* to a *silent* picture.

potential: difference in electrical charge between two points in a *circuit*.

pot(entiometer): round control *console rheostat* raising or lowering *audio* or *video levels*. See: *attenuator*. Compare: *fader*.

POV: (camera's) point of view.

power: *broadcast transmitter output* (in *watts*).

power cord—line cord: electric supply wires.

powerhouse: *radio station licensed* by *FCC* to operate at 50 *kW* on a *frequency* assigned to no other full-time *licensee*. Compare: *CH, daytimer, PSA*.

power pack: rechargeable portable battery power supply for *film* or *tape* camera or *tape recorder,* often belt-mounted. See: *battery belt, nickel-cadmium*.

practical: *set* piece or *prop* that actually works. A *practical lamp* may or may not have some effect on actual *set* illumination.

Praxinoscope: early mirrored-drum *animation* device (Reynaud, 1877). Compare: *Phenakistoscope, Zöetrope*.

preamp(lifier): electronic equipment boosting very weak *signal voltages* to useable *amplifier levels* without additional *signal-to-noise* deterioration.

pre-emptible: *commercial broadcast time* sold at discount by *station* but subject to "recapture" if station finds advertiser willing to pay full *rate*.

pre-emption: optional "recapture" of *network time* by an *affiliate* (or of otherwise-scheduled *network time* by the *network* itself) for special, usually last-minute *programming*. Compare: *acceptance*.

pre-light: arrange *set lighting* in advance of actual *production*.

premium rate: *station's* extra charge for specially requested *commercial time* position. Compare: *ROS*.

premium television: any television *transmission* system charging for *program viewing*. See: *pay cable, pay television, see/fee, STV*.

pre-mix: preliminary *audio mix* reducing quantity of sound elements.

pre-production: all planning activity prior to actual *production*.

pre-record: prepare material for later *playback* during *production*.

pre-score: *record* final *sound* or music *track*, before *filming* or *video taping* to *playback*. Compare: *post score*.

presence: *audio* dimension of realistic immediacy.

preset: store control data for automatic *retrieval*.

pressing: *vinyl (PVC) phonograph* (or *video*) *disk*, mass-produced from molds. Compare: *acetate*.

pressure pad: pad holding *tape* against *record/playback heads*.

pressure plate: *camera* or *projector gate* unit holding film *frame* flatly on *pins* in the *focal plane*. Compare: *claw*.

pressure roller—pinch roller—puck: rubber idler wheel holding recording *tape* against *capstan spindle* during *transport*.

presynchronization: usually, *pre-recording* voice *tracks* for lip-movement *animation*.

preview: *control room monitor* showing upcoming *scenes, effects, titling*, etc. Compare: *line monitor*.

primary colors: (not the artist's opaque pigments red, yellow and blue, but optically—and electronically) red-orange, green and blue-violet. No mixture of any two can produce the third. See: *additive primaries, RGB, triad*. Compare: *subtractive primaries*.

prime lens: *lens* of fixed *focal length*. Compare: *zoom lens*.

prime time: four hours of a *station's broadcast schedule* attracting peak audiences, traditionally from 7:00 P.M. to 11:00 P.M. (advanced one hour in Central and Mountain Time Zones). Under a 1971 *FCC* ruling, only three hours of this period— generally 8:00 to 11:00 P.M.—may be used for *network*-fed television *programming*. See: *time*.

Prime Time Access Rule—PTAR (I, II, III): October 1, 1971 *FCC* ruling reducing *network prime time feeds* to top-50-market *affiliates* to a total of three hours per evening (with waivers), aimed at forcing more local television *programming*. (After October 1, 1972, this local *programming* could not include either *network* or film *re-runs*.) See: *"Westing-*

house Rule." (Modified 1974 and after to return 7:00 P.M. to 7:30 P.M. period for *network* feeds.)

print: *positive* copy from a *film negative* that duplicates original subject tonal values and/or colors. Also: *Film director's* call to include completed *take* in next day's *rushes*. See: *buy.* Also: Space advertising in newspapers and magazines.

printed circuit: metal *conductor* path etched onto laminated plastic base.

printer: optical duplicating machine exposing *positive film print* stock to light through a *negative image,* or vice versa.

printing light: calibrated amount of illumination used to print a particular *film scene.* See: *cinex.*

printing sync: *synchronization* of picture and *soundtrack* to allow for *pullup track* delay. Compare: *cutting sync.*

print-through: excessive magnetism transferred from one *audio tape* layer to the next, producing a "ghost" sound. Usually caused by *overloaded recording levels,* high *tape* storage temperatures, or physical shock.

print-up (print-down): decreasing (increasing) density of *optical soundtrack* for dramatic *volume* increases (decreases).

prism block: compact color-separating optical unit.

prism lens: optical device producing "in camera" multiple images.

probability sample—random sample: research units mechanically selected for statistical projection.

proc amp—video processing amplifier: electronic device to alter *video signal* (*sync,* picture, color) characteristics.

processing: *developing,* fixing, washing, drying and *printing negative film.* See: *laboratory.*

process shot: optical combination of *film images* to make them appear photographed by a single camera. See: *blue matteing, rotoscoping.* Compare: *chromakey.*

producer: in-charge person preparing any project for *broadcast production* and directly responsible for its economic success or failure.

production: preparation of *program* or *commercial* material for *broadcast.*

production assistant: *producer's* general assistant. See: *gopher*.

production house: specialist facility to prepare *film* or *video tape commercials*.

production secretary: in Britain, *director's* personal assistant.

product protection—commercial protection: *broadcast station's* formal minimum time interval between competing *commercial* messages. See: *separation*.

profile—demographics: breakdown of *broadcast* audiences by varying statistical characteristics, such as sex, age, family size, education and economic level. See: *audience composition*. Compare: *psychographics*. Also: **profile:** dimensional free-standing piece of "landscape" *scenery*. Compare: *drop*. Also: Minute-by-minute *program* audience *viewing* pattern.

program: computer processing instructions. Also: *Sponsored* or un-*sponsored broadcast* presentation.

projectionist: *projector* operator. Compare: *VTR operator*.

projector: machine for passing *focussed* high-intensity light beam through *motion picture film* onto distant reflective *screen*, usually simultaneously reproducing *film's synchronized soundtrack*. Compare: *VTR*.

Project Sanguine: abandoned plan for 20,000 sq. mi. underground *antenna* plus 100 buried *transmitters* to bounce *ELF* (45–60 *Hz*) *waves* off the *ionosphere* and into the ocean for emergency U.S. Navy communication with submerged nuclear submarines.

Project Seafarer: revised half-billion dollar version of *Project Sanguine* (above); suggesting only 3,500 sq. mi. of buried *antenna* with seven above-ground *transmitters* (now also abandoned).

Project Westford: 1963 *NASA* stratospheric *grid* of 400 million copper wires for reflective space communication.

promo(tional announcement): *network* or *station commercial* announcement of forthcoming *program*. See: *clutter*.

prompter: device rolling up a large *script* in the performer's view. When mounted above a camera, performer reads (by way of 45° half-silvered mirror) while looking directly into *lens*.

Called *autocue* in Britain. Compare: *cue card*. Also: In Britain, *microphone/speaker* system connecting *studio* to *control room*.

prop list—prop plot: list of required *production properties*.

props—properties: owned or rented non-structural *set* furnishings.

protection: reproducible *duplicate* in event of damage to *master*. In film, *interpositive* struck from *optical negative;* in *video tape*, first *duplicate* off air *master*. Called *backing copy* in Britain. Compare: *composite master*. Also: Wide camera position to cover *jump cuts* of *lip-sync close-ups*. See: *insurance*.

proxar: supplemental screw-on *close-up* element(s) to shorten *lens focal length*. See: *diopter lens, extension tube, lens extender*.

PSA—public service announcement: *broadcast time* contributed by *station* for messages of noncommercial nature. Also: **pre-sunrise authority:** special *FCC* authorization to *day-timer radio station* for early *sign-on*.

PSSC—Public Service Satellite Consortium: non-profit organization established March, 1975 to utilize *NASA satellite transmissions* for public service. See: *ATS-6*.

psychographics: audience research in personality characteristics and attitudes. Compare: *demographics*.

PTAR: see *Prime Time Access Rule*.

public access: cable *channel*(s) reserved for individuals' *programming* at minimal *facilities* fees. *On-air* version called *open door* in Britain.

"public interest, convenience and necessity": traditional catchwords of Federal Communications Act of 1934, describing operational standard for U.S. *broadcast station licensees*.

puck—pinch roller—pressure roller: rubber idler wheel holding recording *tape* against *capstan spindle* during *transport*.

pull back: *dolly* camera away from subject. Compare: *push in, zoom*.

pull down: *camera/projector* action moving *film* into *gate* one *frame* at a time by means of a *claw*. Compare: *pullup*.

pull focus: in Britain, alter *focus* to another subject.

pull negative: *match original negative film* to *edited work print.*

pull the breakers: in Britain, go on strike.

pullup: *loop* of *film* (approximately one second long) in *film projection path* to snub intermittent jerking through *picture gate* into required smooth flow over *sound head;* 20-frame *loop* in *35mm,* 26 frames in *16mm* (optical: 28 frames magnetic); 52 frames (2.17 seconds) in *8mm.* Compare: *pull down.*

Pulse: in-home aided recall *radio* audience survey service. Compare: *National Arbitron.* Also: **pulse:** electronic *signal* variation of finite *amplitude* and duration generated for control reference or *circuit* activation.

pulsed magnetron: British (WW II) *radar* device generating *microwaves* 10 centimeters long, at 3,000 *megacycles.*

pumpkin: *animation stand* projection of television *picture safety* area.

punch: *film cue* created by hole-punch, used visually when *recording* against *picture.* Compare: *beep.*

punch up: switch to a specific *feed.*

pup—baby: 500-*watt spotlight.*

purchase proposition: basic creative *copy* summarizing putative product differences. See: *position.*

pure tone: single *frequency* sound without overtones.

purity: degree of *video* color separation; registration maintained by tri-color *beam* control coil.

push—force: develop *film emulsion* beyond its recommended *exposure rating,* usually half or full *stop.*

push in: *dolly* camera towards subject. Compare: *zoom.*

PVC: see *vinyl.*

Q

Q signal ("quadruture" signal): purple-to-yellow/green *chrominance sideband* (3.58 *MHz*) produced by *subcarrier modulation* phased 147° from *color burst* reference. See: *I signal*. Compare: *Y signal*.

QS: *CBS*-pioneered *matrix quadruphonic* system. Compare: *SQ*.

quad—quadruplex: four-unit *video tape recording* (and *playback*) *headwheel*, rotating (14,400 *rpm*) at right angles to *transported 2″ tape*, "writing" *video* information in successive almost-vertical stripes (1,2,3,4,1,2,3,4, etc.). Called *four-H* in Britain. Compare: *helical scan*.

quadlite: unit containing four 500-*watt floodlights*.

quadruphonic: *FM broadcast* or home *recording* system utilizing four *loudspeakers*, two in front and two behind listener. Compare: *stereophonic*.

quadruture error: *video recording head* mis*alignment*.

quantity discount: see *frequency discount*.

quartz-iodine—Q-I: *tungsten-halogen lamp* (3,200–3,400°*K*) containing iodine gas in a quartz envelope; 650*w*, 750*w*, 1*K* (*redhead*), 2*K* (*blonde*).

quick cuts: instantaneous picture changes (without *dissolves*).

quick study: performer able to memorize lines rapidly.

quintile: standard television audience research size factor.

quonking: accidental sounds picked up by open *microphone*.

R

RAB—Radio Advertising Bureau: *radio* advertising trade development organization. Compare: *TVB*.

rabbit ears: V-shaped in-home television *antenna*.

raceway: recessed *cable* channel.

rack: pivot a *camera lens turret*. Also: Mount *reels* and *thread film* into *projection path*. Also: In Britain, register *film* in *projector gate*. Also: Sorting *pin* bar above editing *bin*. Also: Instrument or equipment mounting frame. See: *bay*.

rack focus: alter *focus* to another subject. Called *pull focus* in Britain.

rack over: shift non-*reflex* camera *lens* into *viewfinder* position.

radar: (*ra*dio *d*etecting *a*nd *r*anging) device generating *microwaves* reflected by target (first moon contact January, 1946: $384,402 \pm 1.5$ km).

RADAR—Radio's All-Dimension Audience Research: British *radio* audience survey. Compare: *JICRAR*.

radio: (Latin: "to radiate") technique for electromagnetic *transmission* of *sound,* based on *wave* theories originated by *Clerk Maxwell* in 1867, developed by *Hertz* in 1885, applied experimentally by *Marconi* in 1895, and utilized in *DeForest's* pioneer Caruso *broadcast* of 1910. Second only to television as most effective means of modern mass communication.

Radio Act: first U.S. government legislation to control domestic *radio* (1912). Compare: *FCC, Federal Radio Act*.

Radio Canada—French side: Quebec Province French-language operation of *CBC*.

Radio Free Europe—Radio Liberty: news and analysis *broadcasting* in 25 languages aimed at the Soviet bloc. Covertly financed ($60 million annually) since 1950's by *CIA*.

radio home: *household* containing one or more *radio receivers*.

radio mike: in Britain, performer's concealed *microphone broadcasting* voice *signal* directly to *receiver/recorder*.

radio spectrum: *frequencies* from 25,000 to 50 billion *Hz*, equivalent of 21 octaves (visible light covers one octave).

radiotelegraphy: *Morse code broadcasting*, initiated by *Marconi* with one-mile *transmission* (1895).

radiotelephony: speech broadcasting, initiated with *DeForest's audion* tube, 1915.

radio telescope: giant *dish antenna* intercepting weak extraterrestrial *radio signals*. See: *SETI*.

radio wave—long wave: *electromagnetic radiation* over 60 meters long, traveling in space at speed of light. See: *short wave*.

RAI—Radiotelevisione Italiana: Italian state-controlled *broadcasting network*. Compare: *BBC, FCC, ORTF, RIAS*.

random access: easy *retrieval* of stored information.

random interlace: imprecise sequential *scanning* of *picture tube field lines*. Compare: *positive interlace*.

random sample—probability sample: research units mechanically selected for statistical projection.

range extender: see *extension tube*.

raster: *picture tube scanned* area, partly hidden by *receiver mask*.

rate card—card rate: *broadcast station's* standard advertising charges, broken down by *time* of day, length of message, and *frequency* of *insertion*. Loosely, to pay this full *rate* with no discount.

rateholder: minor advertising announcement, *broadcast* only to maintain *sponsor's* weekly *schedule* continuity and discount structure. See: *short rate*.

rating: size of potential or actual *broadcast* audience. (*ARB* Rating

Number totals estimated local *households* viewing a *telecast* during an average quarter hour of the reported *transmission* period; *AA Rating* is percentage of national *television homes viewing* average *telecast* minute.) See: *hypo.* Compare: *share.* Also: *Film emulsion speed* index number. See: *DIN, A(N)SI.* Also: *Circuit* or equipment *load* design capacity.

rating book: bi-weekly subscription booklet containing audience measurements. Loosely, the bi-weekly period itself. See: *Nielsen, NTI.*

rating point—point: *broadcast* audience size standard. See: *gross rating points, net rating points.*

rating service: research organization offering periodic audience survey measurements.

ratio—editing ratio: relationship of *exposed film stock* to final *edited footage;* average around 7 to 1. Called *cutting ratio* in Britain. Also: See *aspect ratio.*

raw stock: unexposed *negative film* or *virgin video tape.*

RCA Corporation (formerly *Radio Corporation of America*): U.S. electronics industry conglomerate.

RDD—random digit dialing: telephone audience survey technique, presumably unweighted because of random access to unlisted subscribers.

reach—cumulative audience—cume: number of unduplicated *broadcast program* (or *commercial*) viewers over specific number of weeks. Compare: *frequency.*

reaction shot: cut to performer's emotional facial response. Compare: *cutaway.*

(sound) reader: *editing* device with *speaker/synchronizer playback head* reproducing *magnetic soundtrack.*

reading: actors' first script rundown. Also: *Animation frame* count.

readout: *retrieval* of stored information, usually in visual display form (see *nixie*) or *hard copy.*

real time: original time span, without compression or selective condensation. Compare: *subjective.*

rear projection: inverted (right for left) *film print projected* through *translucent screen.*

rear (screen) projection—RP: *projection* of *still* or *motion picture* as scenic *background*. Normally used for scenes where background area is relatively small—e.g., looking through a car or room window. Called *back projection* in Britain. Compare: *background projector, front (axial) projection.*

recall interview: telephone audience survey technique researching recent *viewing*/listening. (Misses homes without phones.)

recce—reccy: in Britain, *pre-production* assessment of proposed *remote broadcast location.*

receiver: combination of electronic equipment to *view* and/or hear a *broadcast*. See: *set*. Compare: *amplifier, tuner.*

receptacle: power outlet.

record: store electromagnetic *signals* for later *retrieval*. Also: *grooved phonograph disk.*

record button: red plastic "lock" under every *video cassette;* its removal deactivates *re-record* capability. Compare: *knock-out tabs.*

record head: *magnetic gap(s)* in *tape path* to *record* picture and/or *sound* information by realigning magnetic particles. Compare: *erase head.*

recording studio: soundproofed room for *audio recording.*

recordist: in Britain, *audio* engineer in charge of *mixing* session.

rectifier: *AC* to *DC* conversion device. Compare: *inverter.*

Red Channels: *broadcasting's* notorious 1950's political blacklist. Compare: *Red Network.*

redhead: 1*K quartz-iodine lamp.*

Red Lion (Pa.): 1969 Supreme Court decision affirming *FCC fairness doctrine.*

Red Network: early *NBC* radio *hookup*. Compare: *Red Channels, Blue Network.*

reduction print: sub*standard*-width *film print*, projected down from larger *negative*—usually *35mm* to *16mm*. (Accompanying *soundtrack* is usually *contact-printed* from a same-sized *track negative*.)

redundancy: backup equipment performing identical function.

reel: flanged metal/plastic hub for winding and storing *film* and *tape*. Reel capacity is usually 1,000 feet for *35mm film*, 400 feet for *16mm* (both slightly over 11 minutes). Standard 2″

video tape reel holds 4,800 feet (64 minutes). Standard ¼″ *audio tape* reels hold 2,400 feet (10″ reel), 1,200 feet (7″ reel), 600 feet (5″ reel). Called *spool* in Britain.

reel-to-reel—open reel: tape *transport* system with separated supply (*feed*) and *take-up reels.* Compare: *cartridge, cassette.*

re-entry: production of additional *switcher effects* as part of original *effect.* See: *double re-entry.*

reference black: minimal (0.014*v*) *signal* separating black television picture *levels* from *sync signals.* Compare: *black level, reference white.*

reference white: brightest part of a television picture, *transmitted* at 100% *voltage* (1.0*v*) with a recommended maximum reflectance value of 60%. Compare: *reference black.*

reflection: any indirect illumination made visible by secondary surface.

reflector: large mirror-like device (with different reflective characteristics on opposite sides) to re-direct *location* sunlight. Compare: *butterfly.*

reflex: optical mirror system permitting through-the-camera-lens viewing of *filmed* subject.

reflex (axial) projection: in Britain, scenic *background* effect, achieved by low-intensity *projection* of *location slides* or *film* along the taking-*lens* axis (by 45° half-silvered mirror) directly on performers and on huge *Scotchlite* screen behind them. Compare: *back (screen) projection.*

regional: *network feed* to and within a specific U.S. geographical area, usually sponsored by advertisers with products not yet in national distribution. Compare: *basic network.*

registration: proper *alignment* of (1) visual elements, (2) separate *images* of a color television camera, (3) *animation cels,* etc.

registration pins—pilot pins: See: *pins.*

rehearse: practice performance.

relay: point-to-point pickup and re-*transmission* system, usually *amplifying* original *signal.*

release: legal permission (or form on which it is executed). Also: News information provided by the subject.

release print: *duplicate tape* or *film* for *air* use. Called *show print* in Britain. Compare: *answer print.*

reluctance: durable but low-quality *microphone.*

Rembrandt lighting: in Britain, 45° angling of *key light* to subject.

remote: *location broadcast.* See: *nemo, survey.* Called *OB* in Britain.

remote truck: self-contained *control room-*and-equipment *broadcast* vehicle, usually with *microwave* capacity. Called *OB van* in Britain.

renewal: contract extension on or before expiration. Also: Regranted *FCC station license.*

rep: see *station rep.*

repeat: *rebroadcast program* or series. Also: Re-exposure of *animation cel cycle;* walking, running, etc.

repeater: *signal* ''way-station'' to provide *amplification* of *transmitted* material.

reportage: blend of *documentary* and *cinéma vérité* production.

report sheet: in Britain, camera operator's *take-by-take* record, with instructions to *laboratory.* Also called *camera sheet, dope sheet.*

reprint: make additional *positive film print* from *negative.*

reproducer: obsolete term for *phonograph pickup.*

reproduction: transformation of *recorded signals* into audible *sound.* Also: Generally, *duplication* of original material.

re-record: *duplicate* previously *recorded* magnetic impulses.

re-run—rebroadcast: repeated *program* material.

residual: *talent* re-use payment. Compare: *buyout, session fee.*

resistance: opposition in *conductor* to passage of steady electric *current.* See: *impedance, ohm.*

resolution: distinguishable television picture detail.

resonance: sound tone reinforcement by identical *frequency* from another source. Also: Natural *frequency* of vibrating body.

response: equipment *output* characteristics.

restore the loop: see *lose the loop.*

resumé: personal employment history.

retail rate: lower *broadcast* advertising *time rate* for local merchants. Compare: *national.*

retained image: see *burn-in.*

re-take: reshoot rejected material.

reticulation: undesirable *film emulsion* wrinkling.

reticule: etched indications on camera *viewfinder* glass indicating unmasked, *projection* (or television *transmission*) "safe" areas. See: *Academy aperture, safety.* Compare: *cutoff.*

retrace: *scanning beam*'s l. to r. return for each successive *horizontal scan line* (in 10.5 *microseconds*).

retrieval: recovery of stored magnetic information.

return: 90° (scenery) *flat* angle.

Reuters: subscriber news service for *broadcast stations,* newspapers. Compare: *AP, UPI.*

reveal: widen (pull back from) camera position to include additional important picture information.

reverb(eration): multiple ˙echo effect added electronically (or acoustically) to an *audio signal.*

reverberation time: time in which *sound level* diminishes to one-millionth of its original intensity.

reversal—direct positive: *camera-original film* producing *positive* image when developed, eliminating intermediate *negative* and *printing* steps.

reverse action: shoot or print normal *film* action "backwards" *frame-by-frame* for special visual *effect.* See: *scratch off.*

rewind: high-speed return of *film* or *tape* from *take-up* to *feed reel.*

rewinds: pair of geared hand-cranked devices spooling off or rewinding *film reels.* See: *tightwinder.*

rf—radio frequency: waves transmitting *video* and/or *audio* electronic *signals.* Compare: *af, if.*

rf modulator: portable-*VTR* device to feed *recorder playback signal* into locally-vacant *television receiver channel.*

rf pattern: "herringbone" television picture *distortion* created by high-frequency *interference.*

RGB: television's red-orange, green and blue-violet channels. See: *additive primaries, primary colors, triad.*

rheostat: wire coil tappable at any point to adjust circuit resistance. Compare: *SCR.*

rhubarb: in Britain, crowd murmurs.

rhythm & blues: *radio station format* featuring contemporary music with emphasis on black performers.

RIAS: *R*adio *I*n the *A*merican *S*ector (of Berlin). Compare: *RAI*.

ribbon: highly sensitive electromagnetic *directional microphone*.

ride gain—ride the needle: *monitor recording* or *transmission levels*.

rifle—shotgun: long, highly *directional microphone*.

rig: set up equipment. Also: *Mobile unit*.

rights: creative or performance equities. See: *license, royalty*.

rimlight: illumination from high behind camera subject. See: *backlight*. Compare: *key, fill light*.

ringing: dark outlines around (usually *matted*) elements in television picture.

rip and read: read news material on air directly from teletype machine.

ripple: *optical effect* producing wavy or "melting" *film dissolve*. Also: *Amplitude* variations in power supply *output*.

ripple tray: shallow reflecting pan containing water and bits of broken mirror.

riser: low *set* platform. Called *block* in Britain. Compare: *apple, pancake*.

rise time: period required to charge an electrical potential.

roadblocking: *scheduling* identical advertising message on all local *broadcast* facilities in same *time* period. Compare: *counterprogramming, horizontal* and *vertical saturation*.

rock: to move *tape* manually back and forth across *playback head*, locating specific *recorded* material.

rock 'n' roll: in Britain, *film audio mixing* equipment permitting easy forward/backwards movement without complete rewinding of *mix* materials.

Roget, Peter Mark: "Thesaurus" compiler and developer of theory of *persistence of vision* (1824).

roll: aberrant vertical television picture movement. Also: Voice *cue* to start *film* or *tape* ("Roll 'em!"). Also: Length of *raw stock* on *core,* usually 1,000 feet of *35mm* or 400 feet of *16mm* film. Also: In Britain, drum-mounted *program credits*.

roll off: eliminate *high* or *low frequencies* (or both) from an *audio signal*. Called *cut off* in Britain.

roll out: move product (and advertising) into new markets.

roll over: television picture effect of *unsynchronized edit*.

room tone: recorded ambient noise, used when spacing (opening up) *soundtracks*. Called *buzz track* and *atmosphere* in Britain.

ROS—run of schedule: *broadcast* advertising *scheduling* left to *station* discretion. *Rates* are lower, but *spots* are *pre-emptible*. See: *BTA*.

rostrum: in Britain, *motion picture* camera mounted vertically over horizontal subject table for single-*frame exposures;* movements of both camera and table are carefully coordinated. See: *animation camera*.

rotoscope: individually-inked "traveling" action *mattes,* changing shape from *frame* to *frame*. Compare: *blue matteing, traveling matte*.

rough cut: initial *work picture assembly* in approximate length and order, with *opticals* indicated by *china marker*. Compare: *fine cut*.

royalty: compensation for use of a creative *equity*. See: *rights*. Compare: *license, PD*.

RP: see *rear (screen) projection*.

rpm—revolutions per minute: *phonograph disk* rotation speed standard.

RTI—radiation transfer index: relative loss of transmitted *fiber optics* light after coupling and propagation.

RTNDA—Radio/Television News Directors Association: professional membership organization.

RTS—Royal Television Society: British professional membership organization.

rumble: motor vibration transmitted at low *frequencies* from *phonograph turntable* through *pickup*.

run: schedule or *transmit program*.

runaway: *production* specifically organized to escape normal union *talent* or *crew* jurisdiction.

rundown: program event order.

runners: in Britain, metal girders suspending lights, etc. over *set*. See: *gantry*.

running part: continuous role in daily dramatic television *program*.

running shot: camera and subject maintain the same relative motion against background.

running time: *broadcast* length.

run-through: cast *rehearsal* without technical *facilities*. Compare: *dry run, dress*.

run-up: *film reel projection* changeover procedure. Also: In Britain, time required to bring *film cameras* or *tape recorders* up to normal operating *speed*.

rushes—dailies: film positives processed overnight from previous day's original *negative* photography. See: *one-light*.

S

SABRE—Steerable Adaptive Broadcast Reception Equipment: low-*interference* British *UHF* receiving *aerial*.

safelight: *darkroom* illumination on *wavelength* not affecting photographic *emulsions*.

safety: *unmasked* area of *transmitted* television picture. (More critical *lettering safety* denotes slightly smaller area than *picture safety*.) See: *Academy aperture, reticule*. Compare: *cutoff*.

SAG—Screen Actors' Guild: *film* performers' union. Compare: *AFTRA*.

sales: *broadcast station's* marketing group.

sample: elementary units selected from a statistical population for research projection.

sandbag: sand-filled heavy canvas bag used to weight *set*-stand legs, etc. Compare: *water bag*.

Sanyo: major Japanese electronics manufacturer.

satellite: orbiting space station for relaying distant television *signals* in ¼ second. Average life about seven years. Initiated with *Telstar* in 1962. See: *Comsat, earth station, Intelsat*. Compare: *antenna, balloon, microwave*. Also: Separate television *broadcast* facility re-transmitting *air* material of nearby *station* to increase its local *coverage*.

SatCom: two *RCA geosynchronous* U.S. communications *satellites* ("F1, F2"), the first launched in 1974. Extensively used by *pay cable*. Compare: *Westar*.

Saticon: improved television camera *pickup tube* with selenium arsenic tellurium *target* surface coating; offers low *lag*, approximately 1-*gamma*, good sensitivity.

saturation: heavy bombardment of *broadcast* audiences with an advertising message. Also: *Intensity* of picture color. See: *autochroma, chroma.* Compare: *brightness range, contrast, hue.*

SAWA—Screen Advertising World Association: trade group promoting *film* advertising in theatres, holding an annual festival.

SBS—Satellite Business Systems: 11 to 14 billion *Hz digital* communications network (on-line by 1980) co-established by IBM, *Comsat* General and Aetna Insurance.

scale: minimum union pay rates.

scallop: wavy television *picture distortion* caused by improper *VTR* vertical *vacuum guide alignment.*

scan: (based on principles enunciated by LeBlanc in 1880) horizontal *electron beam sweep* across the television camera *target* or *picture tube* in $^1/_{15}$ *millisecond.* Full vertical *scan* in U.S. is $^1/_{60}$ second, in Britain, $^1/_{50}$.

scanning: converting *film* to electronic *signal.*

scanning disk: mechanical television system invented by Nipkow in 1884.

scan(ning) line: single horizontal path traced across *television picture tube* by *electron beam.* See: *blanking interval.*

scanning spot beam: experimental *satellite* communications system *broadcasting* "bursts" of information at 600 million *bits* per second over multiple 10,000 sq. mi. areas.

scatter plan: carefully random *broadcast* advertising *schedule* for audience maximization.

scene: *setting* for particular piece of *action*, usually with single camera *set-up.*

scenery: *set* pieces to suggest real (usually interior) *location.*

SCG—Screen Cartoonists Guild: *animation* workers' union.

schedule: dates and *times* of advertiser's *broadcast* commitments. See: *media, time buyer.* Compare: *campaign.*

schematic: electronic equipment wiring diagram.

Schlieren lens: optical device for *video projection*.

Schmidt mirror: optical device for *video projection*.

schtick: unusual personal routine.

sciopticon: theatrical device projecting a moving *slide*.

scoop—basher: 500-*watt* circular *floodlight*.

scope—oscilloscope: *cathode-ray tube* device for visual electronic *signal* analysis.

score: write music against picture. Also: Musical portion of a *program*.

Scotchlite: proprietary highly-reflective *background* sheeting.

scouting—location scouting—survey: *pre-production* assessment of proposed *remote broadcast* site. Called *recce* or *reccy* in Britain (for *reconnaissance*).

SCR—silicon-controlled rectifier: *solid-state semi-conductor*, basis for most modern *dimmers*. Compare: *rheostat*.

scramble/unscramble: *encode/decode* electronic *signal transmission*.

scrambled: jumbled *pay-television transmission*.

scraper: knifelike *splicer* device removing *film emulsion* preparatory to applying *cement*.

scratch: transverse mechanical damage to *oxide* coating of *video tape*, resulting in *playback dropouts*. Also: Similar damage to *negative* (white scratch) or *positive* (black scratch) *film*.

scratch off: *animation film effect*, photographed (not *printed*) backwards to make removed material "appear." See: *reverse action*.

scratch print: sample *positive stock shot* deliberately damaged to prevent illicit *duplication*, with original *negative* maintained intact for subsequent *print* order and *duplication*.

scratch track—guide track: temporary *soundtrack* prepared to assist *editing* or subsequent *silent camera work*.

screen: reflective surface for *film projection*. Also: *Phosphorescent* inner surface of *CRT* or television *picture tube*.

screen ratio: see *aspect ratio*.

scrim: gauze (or metal) light *diffuser*. See: *butterfly, silk, spun*. Also: Gauze stage curtain.

script: material written for *broadcast* performers to read or act.

script girl: recording clerk of all *set* action. Called *continuity girl* in Britain.

scriptwriter: professional *broadcast* writer. See: *continuity*.

SE—SFX: *sound effects*. Compare: *effects, FX*.

SEC—secondary electron conduction: television *camera pickup tube* designed for low light *levels*. Compare: *image, isocon, SIT*.

SECAM—sequential couleur à mèmoire: French, Soviet and Eastern European television color *transmission* standard (625 line, 50 field); operationally, the world's simplest system—less demanding in terms of timing accuracy and least subject to *color signal distortion*. (Occasionally identified as "*s*ystem *e*vidently *c*ontradicting *A*merican *m*ethod.") Compare: *NTSC, PAL*.

secondary service: see *skywave*.

second generation: see *generation*.

Section 315: see *Equal Time*.

Section 326: "free speech" portion of Federal Communications Act of 1934, prohibiting *FCC censorship*.

see/fee: pay (per *program*) *cable* television. See: *pay cable, premium television*. Compare: *pay television, STV*.

SEG—Screen Extras Guild: film *extras'* union. Also: *Special effects* generator. See: *matteing amplifier*.

segmented: *"Type B"* 1" *video tape* format (*Bosch*) recording each television *frame* in 51 short tracks; *freeze*-framing only with *framestore* attachment. Compare: *non-segmented, single-scan*.

segué: (musical term = "follow up.") "dissolve" from one *audio* element into another. Compare: *cut*.

SelectaVision: RCA *video disk recording* system.

selected take: approved version of *taped* or *filmed scene*. See: *buy*. Compare: *hold, outtake*.

selectivity: *receiver* (*tuner*) discrimination between two adjacent *broadcast signals*.

selenium: light-sensitive element (electrical properties discovered by May in 1873).

self-matteing: *film optical* process utilizing color *mattes* to eliminate *rotoscoping*. Compare: *chromakey*.

selsyn—self-synchronous: *servo* control maintaining two motors at same speed.

semi-conductor: material capable of electron transfer (by free electrons in its molecular structure) upon application of tiny *voltages.* See: *chip, integrated circuit, microprocessor.*

senior: 5,000 *watt spotlight.* Also called *five* or *5K.* Compare: *junior.*

sensitometer: *film emulsion speed* measurement device. Compare: *densitometer.*

separation: protective time period between competitive *commercials.* See: *product protection.* Also: Breakdown into *primary colors.* Also: *Decibel* ratio between *speaker channels.*

separation positives—color separations: three separate *b/w film* records of each of the three primary components of a color *negative,* for protection and *optical* work.

serial: *across the board soap opera.*

servo: "closed" system utilizing *output* to control *input.*

SESAC (originally *S*ociety for *E*uropean *S*tage *A*uthors and *C*omposers): trade guild protecting musical performance rights. Compare: *ASCAP, BMI.*

session fee: *producer's* payment for initial *talent filming* or *recording* services. Compare: *residual.*

set: *radio receiver*—425 million in U.S. (1978), 115 million outside of homes; television *receiver*—123 million in U.S. (1978— 97% of all homes), 54 million color.

set(ting): *studio* construction to suggest real (usually *interior*) *location.* Compare: *cyc, limbo, no-seam.*

set-and-light: prepare for *studio production.* See: *dress.*

set light: *background* (as opposed to subject) illumination.

SETI—Search for Extraterrestrial Intelligence: *NASA* program broadcasting Earth information into space.

sets-in-use—audience potential: obsolete audience survey count of home *receivers* actually switched on during a specific time period. See: *HUR, HUT.*

set up: position of all *camera* and *recording* equipment, *scenery* and *props* at start of a *shot.*

set-up—pedestal: electronic calibration (interval between *blanking* and *black level pulses*) of television *picture black levels.* (*brightness* control on home *receivers*). See: *blacker than black, reference black.*

7½ ips: *audio tape recording speed,* usually non-professional. Compare: *15 ips.*

750: baby *spotlight.*

78 rpm: obsolete *phonograph disk* rotation speed. See: *shellac.*

SFP—Societé Francaise de Production: French state television production facility (derived from *ORTF*) feeding *channels* TF1, A2, FR3.

SFX—SE: *sound effects.* Compare: *effects, FX.*

shade: degree of black mixed into pure *hue.*

shader—video engineer: technician controlling television picture quality (*black level, color balance, exposure gamma, video gain*) for *switcher.*

shading: television picture *contrast adjustment.*

shadow mask: perforated *mask* directly behind face of color *television picture tube,* separating *RGB* electron *beams.* Compare: *faceplate.*

share—share point: audience survey percentage of *households* actually *viewing station's programming* during an average television minute. Compare: *rating.*

shared I.D.: *station identification* added to *commercial copy* on *slide,* card or *film.*

shared time: simultaneous computer usage by two or more *terminals.*

share the boob: enjoy equal exposure on television.

shash: in Britain, television *picture breakup* caused by weak *video signal* reception.

shellac: obsolete *78 rpm phonograph disk pressing* material.

SHF—super high frequency: *wavelengths* 3–30 *GHz.*

shielded cable: inner *signal conductor* protected (from stray *signals*) by outer *grounded* metallic braid.

shoot: n., a *filming* or *video taping;* v., to *film* or *video tape.* Possibly derived from Marey's 1882 photographic "rifle." See: *shot.*

shooting date: scheduled day of *filming* or *video taping.*

shooting script: numbered *scenes* with technical instructions.

shootoff: excess artwork border insuring *bleed* of camera *image*

short: *program* material hardly filling allotted *time*. Compare: *long, tight*. Also: Accidental electrical *circuit grounding*.

short end: un*exposed film* at *tail* of unloaded *raw stock reel*.

short rate: additional charge when advertiser fails to fulfill contract *rate*. Compare: *rateholder*.

short skip: minimal *transmission signal* reflection (100 to 1,000 miles). See: *skip effect*. Compare: *long skip*.

short wave: *electromagnetic radiation* in space, up to 60 meters long. Compare: *long wave*.

shot: individually photographed *scene*. See: *shoot*.

shot box: pre-set device controlling *zoom lens* system.

shotgun—rifle: long, highly *directional microphone*.

shot list—shot sheet: *live* television cameraman's card listing his shots. Called *crib card* in Britain.

shoulder brace: hand-held body-conforming camera support.

show print: in Britain, *duplicate tape* or *film* for *air* use.

shutter: rotating segmented *disk* in both *film camera* and *projector*. Also: *Spotlight intensity* control.

shutter bar: horizontal line area moving upward in television picture of ordinary *film screen* projection, and vice versa. Called *bar line* in Britain.

shutters: vertical slat *diffusers* affixed to *brute*.

SI: *I*nternational *S*ystem of measurement.

SIA—Storage Instantaneous Audimeter: updated *Nielsen Audimeter* device offering quicker *readout*.

sibilance: voice *tape hiss*.

sideband: *rf-modulated* area above (or duplicated below) *carrier frequency*. Note: In single *sideband transmission,* one *sideband* is suppressed at *transmitter*.

signal: electric impulse derived from and convertible to visible picture and/or audible *sound*.

signal generator: television test *signal* device.

signal-to-noise ratio–S/N–snr: *signal* strength (expressed in *db's*) as a function of extraneous *interference* induced by the *transmission* system itself.

signatory: *producer* formally adhering to *talent* union contract. See: *letter of adherence*.

signature: unique musical device denoting specific product or advertiser.

sign-on—sign-off: *station identification* information *broadcast* at beginning and end of daily *transmission*.

silent: *film* prepared or *projected* without *soundtrack*. Compare: *sound*.

silent speed: 16 *frame-per-second film exposure* rate (meeting all *persistence of vision* requirements). See: *sound speed*.

Silicon Valley: epithet for Santa Clara, California area producing major U.S. share of metal oxide *semi-conductor* memories and silicon *chip microprocessors*.

silk: gauze light *diffuser*. See: *butterfly, scrim, spun*.

silver-oxide battery: button-sized, low power *dry cell*, characterized by long life and sudden failure.

simplex: temporarily replace regular *broadcasting* by another service. Compare: *duplex, multiplex*.

simulcast: simultaneous *television* and *radio program*.

single broad: box-shaped 2,000-*watt fill light*.

single perf(oration): *16mm film* with *soundtrack* along one edge, *sprocket* holes along the other. Compare: *double perf*.

single rate card: *broadcast station's* identical charge for both *national* and local advertising. Compare: *retail rate*.

single-scan—non-segmented: *"Type C"* 1″ *video tape* format (*Ampex, Sony*) *recording* one complete television *field* during each *head* pass; permits *freeze-framing*. Compare: *segmented*.

single sprocket: see *single perf*.

single-strand: successive *negative* sequences *optically printed* onto one piece of *film*.

single system: picture and *sound* simultaneously *recorded* (and *developed*) on same piece of *film* (used primarily in news photography); *pullup* requires pauses at *edits*. Compare: *double system*.

siphoning: (fee) *cable transmission* of *program* originally available by direct (free) *broadcast*.

SIT—silicon-intensified target: television *camera pickup tube* designed for low light *levels;* offers low *lag,* high sensitivity, good *resolution.* Compare: *image isocon, SEC.*

SITE—Satellite Instructional Television Experiment: educational *transmission* by *satellite* (first used in India, 1974).

16mm: *film* stock 16mm wide, adopted as international standard in 1923; 40 *frames* to the foot, 0.6 feet per second at *sound speed* (24 *fps*). Compare: *Super 8, 35mm.*

625-line: standard number of horizontal line *sweeps* per *frame* in all Eastern Hemisphere (except Japan) television *transmission* systems (offering better picture *resolution* than U.S. *525-line*).

skating: unequal *phonograph* record *groove* wear.

skew: zig-zag television picture *distortion* caused by improper *VTR* horizontal vacuum guide *alignment.*

skip effect: long-distance reflection of *radio waves* (sometimes erratic) from *ionosphere.* See: *long skip, short skip.*

skip frame: *printing* every other *frame* to double apparent speed of action. Compare: *double print.*

sky filter: see *haze filter.*

sky pan: *cyclorama floodlight.*

skywave: secondary portion of *broadcast signal* radiating skyward (*AM* reflects from *ionosphere*). Compare: *groundwave.*

slant track: loose term for *helical scan recording.*

slap: in Britain, performer's *makeup.*

slash print: in Britain, quick non-*balanced print* from newly-completed *optical picture negative* to check mechanical *printing* errors. Often used for *dubbing.*

slate: several *frames* of a small blackboard with chalked *scene* information, photographed at start of each *take;* often a hinged *clapstick* provides *double-system synchronization.* Called *ident board, number board, clapper board* or *take board* in Britain. See: *end slate.* Also: Equivalent verbal recorded identification on original *soundtrack;* called *announcement* in Britain.

slave(s): *recorder(s) dubbing playback* from a *master.* Also: *Video tape* so used.

sled: *set luminaire* support.

SLICE—Source Label Identifying and Coding Equipment: in Britain, *IBA* equipment for *transmitting* non-*program* data during television's *vertical blanking interval.* Compare: *ANTIOPE, Ceefax, ORACLE, Teletext, Viewdata.*

slice (of life): television *commercial* creative technique purporting to reflect conversation of real people.

slide: transparent photograph mounted on *drum* and projected into *camera chain* for television *broadcast.*

slide film: sequence of individual 35mm *slides,* shown singly in cartridge *slide projector,* with or without separate *synchronized soundtrack.* Compare: *filmstrip.*

slider: see *fader.*

slop print: see *check print.*

slot: recurring *program* period.

slow (fast): *emulsions* less (or more) sensitive to light. (Slow *emulsions* tend to be less grainy.)

slow-mo: *video disk* equipment (recording 30 seconds of *real time*) for speed-up, *slow motion, freeze frame* or *reverse action* effects (introduced in 1965).

slow motion: apparent slowdown of an action by *film overcranking.* Called *turn fast* in Britain.

slow scan: simplified television *transmission* system for *still* subjects (also used in space exploration).

smear: see *comet tail.*

SMPTE—Society of Motion Picture and Television Engineers—"Simpty": standard-setting professional engineering group. Compare: *IEEE.*

SMPTE standard test bars: see *color bars.*

SMSA—Standard Metropolitan Statistical Area: census market designation.

sneak: slow *sound* or picture *fade-in* or *-out.*

snoot—funnel: conelike or tubelike attachment pinpointing *spotlight beam.*

snorkel: inverted periscopic *lens* system, permitting unusual *close-up* camera perspectives.

snow: television *picture breakup* caused by weak *video signal* reception. Called *shash* in Britain.

soap (opera): *daytime broadcast,* uually highly melodramatic, historically *sponsored* by soap manufacturers.

soapdish: *audio cassette* plastic container.

socket: mechanical *circuit* inter*connector* (*female*). Compare: *plug.*

sodium thiosulfate—hypo: photo developing fixative.

SOF—sound-on-film: *footage* accompanied by *sound,* usually *filmed* by *16mm single-system* camera.

soft: unintentional (or deliberate) lack of sharp *focus.*

soft copy: *readout* on *CRT.* Compare: *hard copy.*

softlite—softlight: *luminaire* providing bright, diffused illumination.

software: *broadcast program* material presented on electronic equipment (*hardware*).

solenoid: electromagnetic switch.

solid state: *transistorized circuit* replacing *vacuum tubes.*

sonic: within audible range (20-20,000 *Hz*). Compare: *infrasonic, ultrasonic.*

sonic cleaner—ultrasonic cleaner: ultra high-frequency *sound wave film* cleaning device.

sonovox: device coupling speech with *sound effects.*

SONY: (from Latin *sonus* = "sound") major Japanese electronics manufacturer.

sound: *film* prepared or projected with *soundtrack.* Compare: *silent.* Also: See *sound wave.*

sound drum: flywheel to insure smooth *film* movement past *projector sound head.*

sound effects—SE—SFX: *recorded* or *live audio* effects creating the illusion of realistic or symbolic sounds. Compare: *EFX, FX.*

sound (effects) man: technician providing *broadcast sound effects.*

sound head: *film projector* system "reading" *optical* or *magnetic soundtrack.*

sound reader: *film editing* device *playing back optical* or *magnetic soundtracks.*

sound report: *film sound* recordist's *take-by-take* record.

sound speed: (*film*) 24 *frame-per-second exposure* rate, offering *high-fidelity sound playback.* Compare: *silent speed.* Also: (Physics) 1,100 feet per second.

sound stage: soundproofed *filming* or *video taping* area in *studio* or *production house.* See: *int.* Compare: *lot.*

soundtrack—track: *audio* portion of *film* or *video tape.*

sound wave: area of air pressure created by any kind of mechanical vibration.

soup: *film developing* solution.

Spanish windlass: in Britain, chain or cable anchoring *tripod* to *stage screw.*

sparkle: white *print* specks = *negative* dirt; black *print* specks = *print* dirt.

sparks: *set* electrician. See: *gaffer.*

speaker—loudspeaker: device *transducing* electronic *signals* into *sound waves.* See: *tweeter, woofer.*

special: *one-shot* major *network program.* See: *blockbuster.* Compare: *across the board, strip.*

special effects: camera illusions. Also: Electronic generation of such graphic elements as *wipes, dissolves, inserts,* etc. See: *matteing amplifier, SEG.*

spec(ification) sheet: technical equipment information.

spectrum: see *electromagnetic spectrum.*

specular: mirror-like reflectance from performer's eyes (or teeth). See: *eye light.*

speed: *film emulsion* light sensitivity. Also: Call when camera or *recording* equipment reaches correct operating rate (see *tape*).

speed up: hand *cue* to increase *talent* speed.

spider: multi-outlet electrical *cable* box. Also: In Britain, metal floor brace for *film camera tripod.* Also: See *spyder.*

spigot: in Britain, threaded *luminaire mounting* pipe.

spike: brief *signal peak transient.*

spill: undesirable illumination.

spill-in: *viewing*/listening audience from outside a *station's ADI* or *DMA.*

spill-out: audience listening/*viewing stations* outside their *ADI* or *DMA.*

spindle: rotating shaft in *tape transport* system. See: *capstan.*

splice: joint between two separate pieces of *tape* or *film.* Called *join* in Britain.

splicer: device for accurate joining of *edited film frames* with transparent tape or *cement.* Called *joiner* in Britain.

splicing block: grooved device to cut and join *audio tape.*

splicing tape: specially-formulated noncreeping pressure sensitive tape applied to base side of *audio tape splice.*

split focus: approximate *focus* between subjects at varying distances from camera.

split reel: reel with unscrewable flange for removing *cored film* without unspooling. Called *split spool* in Britain.

split screen: divided *frame* containing two or more *image* areas.

sponsor: *broadcast* advertiser. See: *account, client.*

spool: in Britain, flanged metal/plastic hub for winding and storing *film* and *video tape.*

spot: colloquial term for any broadcast *commercial* (from the days when the *networks* sold *sponsorships* and only local *stations* sold individual "on the spot" *commercials*). Also: (Spotlight) directional *luminaire* with variable-angle, *focusable* beam.

Spotlight: in Britain, four-volume directory of performing *talent.*

spot television—spot radio: *commercial* time purchased market by market by advertiser with national or regional product distribution.

spotter: sports *announcer's* assistant.

spray: reduce reflected glare with aerosol matte finish. Also: Special *laboratory film developing* process.

spread—stretch: slow down a *broadcast* presentation. Also: Unplanned increase in running time. Also: **spread:** diffuse a *luminaire beam.*

sprocket: toothed gear in *film transport* system, engaging edge perforations (*sprocket* holes). See: *double perf, single perf.*

spud: *luminaire* pipe support. See: *turtle.* Compare: *century stand.*

spun: gauze light *diffuser.* See: *butterfly, scrim, silk.*

Sputnik I: initial (*transmission* only) global *satellite,* launched by U.S.S.R. October 4, 1957. Compare: *Explorer I.*

sputtering: (obsolete) gold surfacing of *acetate phonograph disk recording* prior to *pressing;* replaced by silverplating. Compare: *one-step, two-step.*

spyder: small *camera dolly.* Compare: *crab dolly.*

SQ: Sansui-pioneered *matrix quadruphonic* system. Compare: *QS.*

squeegee: wiping device in continuous *film processor.*

(un)squeeze: (de)*anamorphize* a *film image.*

squelch: *receiver* "gate" *circuitry* eliminating unmodulated signal.

SSI—small-scale integration: five miniaturized *circuits* on one-inch wafer. Compare: *LSI.*

SSPD: self-scanned *photodiode* array.

stability: continuous operating *balance.*

stabilizer: anti-vibration camera *mount.* See: *Steadicam, Tyler mount.*

stage: *studio* production area.

stage brace: *scenery* support strut.

stagehand: general *set* worker. See: *grip.*

stage right, stage left: movement from (camera- or audience-facing) performer's point of view. Compare: *camera right, camera left.*

stage screw: *set* floor anchor for *tripod* chain, etc. See: *Spanish windlass.*

stagger through: in Britain, first *rehearsal* without *costumes, facilities,* etc.

staircase: television test signal measuring *differential gain, phase luminance signal* linearity, and *burst phase* errors.

STAM—sequential thermal anhysteric magnetization: high speed (5 to 1) *helical scan video tape* contact printing *duplication* (discontinued technique). Compare: *AC transfer.*

standard: *35mm film.* Also: Adjustable height *set* support. Also: *AM broadcasting.*

standards conversion: see *converter.*

stand by: *action* warning *cue.*

standby: contingency replacement performer (or *program*). Also: *VTR mode—tape* stationary, *record head(s)* in motion.

stand-in: substitute performer, not recognizable as such if photographed. Compare: *extra, understudy.*

standing set—permanent set: *set* in continuing *production* use. Compare: *strike.*

star—star filter: line-engraved *lens* filter transmitting light source as pointed star effect.

start mark: *synchronization* indication at *head* of *film* and/or *soundtrack.*

stat—photostat: inexpensively-processed photographic reproduction, usually enlarged or reduced from the original to match available space.

static: acoustic noise produced by random energy in a *radio signal.*

station: *broadcasting* facility assigned specific *frequency.* First government authorization (*radio*) issued to WBZ, Springfield, Mass., Sept. 15, 1921. Now over 8,000 U.S. *radio* stations; 900 television (1978).

station break: pause in *program transmission* for *FCC*-required *call-letter* identification, usually at half-hour intervals.

station identification—ID: *10-second commercial* announcement, with *audio* limited to 8 seconds or less to allow for shared station identification. Now any *10-second broadcast* advertising message.

station rep(resentative): group representing local *stations* for sale of *broadcast time* to a national advertiser.

Steadicam: proprietary *servo*-controlled body-mounted *film*-or-television camera. See: *enhanced hand-held.* Compare: *Magicam, minicam.*

Steenbeck: German horizontal *film*-and-*sound editing machine.* See: *Kem, Moviola.*

step on: overlap another performer's lines.

step printer: *film laboratory* machine to print *optical picture negatives.* Compare: *continuous printer.*

steps—test bars: bar-shaped pattern used in *video tape recording* for *playback alignment.* See: *color bars.*

step wedge—wedge—step tablet: length of *motion picture negative* for *processing* control, each *frame* progressively darker. Compare: *camera test, cinex.*

stereo(phonic): "dimensional" *sound* reproduction achieved by use of two separated *recording microphones* matched to similarly separated *playback speakers*. Compare: *quadru-phonic*.

Stereoscope: "depth" *slide* viewer (Wheatstone, 1838).

"sticks": *cameraman's* call for *clapstick sync* action.

stilb: one *candela* (0.8 *foot candle*) of light covering square centimeter of surface.

still: single photograph.

still frame: individual *film* or *video tape frame* held as continuous *shot*. See: *frame-store*.

sting: dramatic single music background note, or chord.

stirrup: device suspending overhead *set luminaire*.

STL: studio-to-transmitter link.

stock—raw stock: unexposed *negative film* or *virgin video tape*.

stock music—library music: previously *recorded background* music *licensed* for re-use. See: *needle drop*.

stock set: standard *scenic background*.

stock shot—library footage: previously photographed *film footage* *licensed* for re-use. See: *scratch print*.

stop: *aperture* opening controlling amount of light passing through *lens* (usually calibrated from 1.5 to 22). See: *f, diaphragm*.

stop down: reduce *aperture* opening.

stop leader: blank *film* indicating *projection* interruption on a single *reel*.

stop motion: *frame*-at-a-time cinematography of three-dimensional subjects moved slightly between exposures; *projection* at *speed* (24 *fps*) gives illusion of actual motion. See: *animation camera*. Compare: *limited animation*.

storage battery: see *battery*.

storyboard: inexpensive stylized format for reviewing all *audio* and representative *video* portions of planned *television commercial;* usually drawn on paper in separated *frames*.

straight across: non-*equalized audio recording*.

straight cut: edit *scene*-to-*scene* with no intervening *optical* device. Compare: *transition*.

straight up: clock second hand at 12.

STRAP—Simultaneous Transmission and Recovery of Alternating Pictures: two television *signals* carried on the same *channel* with independent *receiver* reconstruction.

Stratovision: obsolete wide-area television *signal* distribution technique utilizing airborne *transmitter/antenna*. Compare: *balloon*.

streaking: *television picture distortion* extending objects horizontally beyond their normal boundaries.

streamer: *editor's* lateral *china marker* indication on *work print* (in *projection*, appearing to run across *frame*).

stress marks: in Britain, random vertical black stripes in *film print*, caused by overtight *negative* winding damage.

stretch: slow down a *broadcast* presentation. Also: Exaggerated *animation change*.

stretch print: upgrade *silent footage* to 24 *fps sound projection speed* by *printing* every other *frame* twice.

strike: dismantle a *set* or equipment after *production*. Compare: *load in*. Also: Print a *positive film* from a *negative*. Less often, make a *dupe* from a *master tape*. Also: Appeal to *FCC* to cancel *allocation* application for cause.

stringer: *free-lance* local journalist.

strip: *program broadcast* at same time each weekday. See: *across the board*. Compare: *one shot, special*. Also: Row of lights, usually containing five 1,000-*watt bulbs*. See: *bank*. Also: Remove *insulation*.

stripe—mag(netic) stripe: clear *35mm sprocketed film* with magnetic *oxide* stripe for recording a single *soundtrack*. Called *zonal stripe* in Britain. See: *balance stripe*. Also: To coat a *film print* with a narrow *oxide* band for *track recording* on *single-system playback*.

stripe filter: vertical surface stripes on camera *pickup tube*, breaking up image light into *RGB* components without *dichroic mirrors*.

stripping: *re-running* several years of (originally a) once-a-week *program across the board*.

strobing: transverse or rotary movement of an object in the *film frame* at a speed undesirably counteracting the phenomenon of *persistence of vision* (also results from too-rapid *panning*).

stroboscope—strobe: device emitting light at controlled intervals.

stroboscopic disk: cardboard rotation-speed checking device.

studio: soundproofed room for creating *broadcast* material. Also: Generally, the premises of large *film* or television facility.

stunting: flamboyant special *network programming*.

STV—subscription TV: *transmission* (for a monthly fee) of over-the-air *television signals* to home *receivers*. See: *premium television, pay television*. Compare: *see/fee, pay cable*.

stylus: *needle* for *phonograph disk cutting* or reproduction. Also: A *video disk tracking* technique.

subcarrier: 3.58 *MHz NTSC* color television *signal*. See: *black burst, color burst*.

subjective: time duration felt by audience. Compare: *real time*.

subliminal: *broadcast* advertising allegedly below normal perception thresholds.

subscriber: *cable* customer.

substandard—narrow-gauge: *film* less than *35mm* wide.

subtitle: explanatory *caption* (often a translation of foreign *soundtrack*) at *frame* bottom. Compare: *title*.

subtractive: color *film processing* system removing components from *emulsion* layers during *development*.

subtractive primaries: *cyan, magenta, yellow*.

sucker—limpet: in Britain, rubber suction cup temporarily attaching equipment to any smooth surface.

sun gun: small portable high-intensity *luminaire*.

sunk up: *sound synchronized* to *picture*.

sunshade: see *matte box*.

sunspot: vast (11-year) cyclic disturbance on sun's surface, creating severe *radio wave* disruption on earth.

sun spot—beam projector—parabolic: *spotlight* projecting a narrow, almost parallel light *beam*.

Super 8: enlarged-frame version of older *8mm motion picture film;* 72 *frames* to the foot, 0.325 *feet per second* at *sound speed* (24 *fps*). Compare: *16mm, 35mm*.

superimpose: overlap pictures from two different cameras.

super(imposition): electronic addition of one picture information source (usually *titling*) over another.

supply reel: see *feed reel.*

suppression: reduction of objectionable *frequencies* to acceptable levels.

surface: extraneous *phonograph record* noise.

surround sound: spectacularly artificial method of *quadruphonic audio recording,* effectively ''seating'' the listener in mid-orchestra.

survey—location scouting: *pre-production* assessment of proposed *remote broadcast* site. Called *recce* or *reccy* in Britain (for *reconnaissance*).

sustainer: unsponsored *network* or local *station broadcast.*

swarf: in Britain, filament thrown up by *disk-*cutting *stylus.*

sweep: electronic *picture tube scan.* Also: Small J-shaped *scenery* piece, usually translucent (see: *milk sweep*), eliminating any visual frame of reference. Also: Television audience *rating* measurement week.

sweetening: addition of new or variant singing to existing song *track.* Also: Addition of audience reaction to *soundtrack.*

swinger—flapper: *flat* swung out of path of camera *dolly.*

swish pan—zip pan: image-blurring *pan* shot, usually transitional. Called *flash pan, whip (wizz) pan* in Britain.

switcher: television input control *console* to select or mix *video output.* Also: Technician (*technical director—TD*) operating this equipment. Called *vision mixer* in Britain.

sync generator: electronic pulsing device controlling television *picture scanning.*

sync(hronization): exact *alignment* of *sound* and *picture* elements. Called *laying* in Britain. See: *edit sync, printing sync.* Compare: *wild.* Also: Television *signal* control.

synchronization rights: permission to *animate* to previously *recorded* musical composition.

synchronizer: greared table device for simultaneously *editing film* and *soundtrack.* Called *four way* in Britain.

synchronous demodulation: color *set's I & Q signal* detection.

synchronous motor: *AC* motor with speed exactly governed by *frequency* of applied *voltage.*

sync mark: *editor's synchronizing* point indication.

Syncom: initial experimental *geosynchronous* (equatorial) *satellite,* launched in a 6,830 mph, 22,240-mile high orbit, February 14, 1963.

sync pulse: *voltage pulse* (4.77 *microseconds* long) introduced into *video signal* during *blanking interval* to insure exact *transmission/reception synchronization.* Also: Camera device using inaudible *sound frequencies* to control *recorder speed.* See: *crystal sync.*

sync punch: hole punched in *film soundtrack* as audible *cue* mark. Called *sync plop* in Britain.

sync roll: vertical television *picture roll over* caused by *circuit* interruption.

sync signal: *pulse* controlling *scanning synchronization.*

sync tone: inaudible *high-frequency signal* added during *tape recording* in order to *servo*-drive *playback* equipment at identical speed.

syndication: preparation of *broadcast programming* (usually series) for separate purchase and *air* use by *independent stations.* See: *package.*

synex: see *cinex.*

synthesizer: device for manipulating color television *broadcast signals* for striking visual effects.

system: *closed-circuit* television *transmission* and reception.

T

T: see *T-stop*.

tab: foil-faced sensor attached to *film negative* for *print timing* purposes. Compare: *notch*.

table top—insert: *close-up* camera work with inanimate objects.

tachometer: camera *frame-speed* indicator.

tag: brief *live* announcement added to *recorded commercial*. See: *open end*. Compare: *cut-in*.

tag line: performer's final line.

tail—tail leader: end portion of *film* or *tape reel*. Compare: *head*.

tails out: film (or *tape*) reel requiring *rewinding* before *projection* (or *playback*). Compare: *heads out*.

take board: see *number board*.

"take it away!": traditional *remote audio broadcast cue*.

takes: consecutively numbered attempts at a *filmed* or *taped* performance. See: *buy, hold, selected take*.

take sheets: detailed *production* records kept by *script girl* or *audio* engineer.

take-up: *reel* spooling up *tape* or *film* from *feed reel*.

take-up plate: *editing table* horizontal *take-up reel*.

talent: *broadcast* performer(s).

talent agent: *broadcast* performer's booking representative; usually taking 10% of fee.

talent union: performer's labor organization. See: *AFTRA, SAG, SEG*.

talkback: private *microphone/speaker* system connecting *control room* to *studio*. Also called *prompter* or *fold back* in Britain. Compare: *PA, PL*.

talking book: recorded literary work.

talking clock: obsolete *videotape* (one-second *audio* counts) *cueing* method. Compare: *time code*.

talking heads: poorly-produced television interview.

talk show: *broadcast format* consisting of celebrity conversations, panel discussions, telephone interviews, etc. Also called *chat show* in Britain.

tally light: red light atop television camera indicating when its *shot* is being *transmitted;* often used to *cue* (when extinguished) camera moves. Also called *camera cue* in Britain. Compare: *camera light*.

tape: non-sprocketed plastic ribbon base $^1/_{1,000}''$ thick and $^1/_8''$ to $2''$ wide, coated with metallic *oxide* and *transported* past a magnetic field for electronic *recording* of *sound* and/or television *picture* patterns. *Audio tape recording speeds* are $1\frac{7}{8}$, $3\frac{3}{4}$, $7\frac{1}{2}$ and 15 *inches per second* (*ips*); standard *quad video tape speed,* 15 *ips.*

tape guide: grooved metal alignment post on either side of *magnetic head*.

tape hook: camera attachment used when measuring distance to subject.

tape lifter: metal arm removing *audio tape* from *record/playback heads* in *fast forward/rewind modes*.

tape recorder: (usually *audio*) electronic/mechanical device for *recording* magnetic information on tape for instantaneous *playback*.

tape speed: see *tape*.

target—dot: metal disk used as *flag*.

target—mosaic: light-sensitive camera *pickup tube* storage surface (over 350,000 *photosensitive* dots) scanned by *electron beam*.

target ring: camera *circuit* draining electrons from conductive layer of *vidicon tube*.

TARIF—Technical Apparatus for Rectification of Inferior

Film: *BBC* device for comingling *film* and *video tape* sources without objectionable *color shift*.

TBA—to be announced: undetermined action for a specific time.

TBD—to be determined: undetermined time for a specific action.

T-bone: in Britain, *luminaire mount* on flat metal base.

TD—technical director—switcher: television *video control console* engineer. Called *vision mixer* in Britain.

TEAC: major Japanese electronics manufacturer.

tearing: *horizontal picture aberration* caused by lack of *sweep synchronization*.

technical director: see *TD*.

technical manager: in Britain, "in-charge" television *studio* technician.

Technicolor: *film color separation* process using three *b/w negative* components.

Telco (patch—line—feed): telephone company *cable* connection.

telecast: television *broadcast*.

teleciné—T/C—T/K: television *station film* and *slide projection chain*.

Telefis Eireann: Eire state-controlled television *network*.

Telegraphon: 1898 Poulsen magnetic *audio recorder* using metal ribbon.

telephone coincidental interview: audience survey technique: "Are you *viewing*/listening?" (Poor at early/late hours; misses homes without phones.)

telephone filter: device passing *audio frequencies* between 200–2,700 *Hz* only.

telephone recall interview: audience technique researching recent *viewing*/listening. (Misses homes without phones.)

telephoto: narrow-angle, long *focal length lens* used for distant objects. Compare: *bugeye, diopter lens, fisheye*.

Teleprompter: patented "roll-up" *script cueing* device; if desired, readable (by way of 45° half-silvered mirror) directly "through" camera *lens*. Compare: *cue card*.

telerecording—kinescoping: poor-quality direct *reversal motion picture filming* of television *tube picture*. Also called *kine, TVR*.

· 181 ·

TELESAT: Canadian television *satellite* system, established with *ANIK* I in 1972; first to use lightweight, semi-portable *earth station* pick-ups.

Teletext: in Britain, *BBC/IBA* computer-generated data system (utilizing spare *lines* in *blanking interval*) imposing *digital signal* on normal television *transmission* to be decoded, displayed or stored on home *receiver*. See: *ANTIOPE, Viewdata*. Compare: *Ceefax, ORACLE, SLICE*.

telethon: lengthy (usually fund-raising) entertainment *program*.

television—TV: technique for electronic *transmission* of *pictures*, first proposed by Carey in 1875, Senlecq in 1877, and demonstrated by Nipkow in 1884; now, with accompanying *sound*, the most effective means of modern mass communication. Over 900 *VHF* and *UHF* television *stations* in U.S.

television game: see *video game*.

television home: see *household*.

telly: (chiefly British) abbreviation for the television system.

telop(ticon): television *camera chain* device *transmitting* small (4″ × 5″) opaque art cards. See: *balop*.

Telstar: initial overseas television communications *satellite* with onboard *transponder*, launched in a 15,000 mph low elliptical 157-minute orbit by *Comsat*, January 10, 1962. See: *Early Bird*.

tempex—carnet: European customs form covering temporary equipment importation.

ten: 10-second *commercial* message; in television *film*, offering 8 seconds of *audio*. Also called *ID*. Compare: *minute, thirty, twenty*.

10K: see *brute*.

tenner: heavy-duty *fresnel-lensed spotlight* with 10,000-*watt bulb*.

terahertz—THz: one trillion *hertz*.

terawatt—TW: one trillion *watts*.

terminal: equipment *power* or *signal* connection point. See: *electrode*. Also: Computer *input* location.

termination: *resistance* at the end of any *video signal* (always 75 *ohms*).

test bars—steps: pattern used in *video tape recording* for *playback alignment.* See: *bar test pattern, color bars.*

test (market) commercial: *on-air broadcast* advertising message primarily produced (at full *talent* rates, although in limited markets) for audience research. Often prepared within a curtailed *production* budget.

test pattern: optical chart, checking television camera, *monitor* or *receiver contrast, linearity* and picture *resolution.* See: *limiting resolution.* Also: *Transmission* of same.

tetrode: *amplifying vacuum tube* with two variably-charged wire mesh *grids* controlling electron flow between *negative filament* (*cathode*) and *positive plate.* Compare: *diode, pentode, triode.*

TF—till forbid: *broadcast schedule* with termination date at advertiser's discretion.

TF1: see *SFP.*

thermal imaging: *vidicon camera tube* system responding to subject's radiated heat, not light.

thermoplastic: image-recording technique utilizing electron beam to deform the surface of special plastic film. Compare: *photoplastic.*

thin: insufficiently *exposed negative.* Compare: *dense.*

thirty: 30-second *commercial* message; in television *film,* offering 28 seconds of *audio.* Compare: *minute, twenty, ten.*

35mm: *film stock 35mm* wide, adopted as international standard in 1907; 16 *frames* to the foot, 1 1/2 *feet* per second at *sound speed* (24 *fps*). Compare: *16mm, Super 8.*

Thirty Rock: *Variety's* epithet for New York corporate headquarters of *NBC* (located at 30 Rockefeller Plaza), matching *Black Rock* (*CBS*) and *Hard Rock* (*ABC*).

33 1/3 rpm: standard *phonograph disk* rotation speed.

thread—thread up: *set up film* (or *tape*) in *projection* (or *record/playback*) *path.*

threefold: three hinged *flats.*

throw: distance from *projector lens* to *screen;* distance from *luminaire* to subject.

throw away: underplay in performance.

THS—Thames: one of British *IBA*'s *"Big Five"* (the *Central Companies*).

ticket: loosely, engineer's *FCC* license.

tied-off: locked camera position (without *pan* or *tilt*).

tie-down (chain, cable): anchor connecting *tripod* to *stage screw*.

tight: camera subject *framing* with no top and side room. Compare: *loose*. Also: *Program* material running very close to allotted time. Compare: *long, short*.

tightwinder: *rewind* (*take-up*) attachment centering *film* on *core*.

tilt: camera movement along a vertical *arc,* from a fixed position. Compare: *pan*. Also: Deficient *low-frequency* response.

tilt wedge: accessory increasing normal camera *mount tilt*.

time—day part: *broadcasting* period, usually for *commercial* advertising sale. See: *daytime, drive time, fringe evening time, prime time*.

time base corrector: *video tape recorder playback circuitry* generating perfect *picture sweep synchronization*.

timebase stability: degree of regularity of *video tape head* drive *servo signal* (*quadruplex,* every 1/2,000 second; *helical scan,* every 1/30 second).

time buyer: *agency* employee purchasing *client's broadcast* advertising periods. See: *media, schedule*.

time check: clock synchronization.

time code—edit code: *SMPTE* standard *video tape retrieval* system (similar to *motion picture edge number* identification) usually recording eight-digit *address* (hours, minutes, seconds, *frames*) on *control track*. See: *address code*. Compare: *talking clock*.

time division multiple access: computerized *millisecond* transmitted-*signal* analysis permitting optimum *channel* sharing.

time lapse: single-*frame* photography at precise periodic intervals. Also: Story break, usually indicated by *optical dissolve*.

time slot: broadcast period. See: *slot*.

timing: subjective alteration of *printing light intensities* and *color filters* to achieve a *balanced film positive* from *unbalanced negative* material.

tinny: lacking in *low frequencies*.

Time Standard: The amount of time to be used for advertising within any clock hour (NAB Radio Code, 18 min/hr 1960

tint: degree of white mixed into pure *hue*.

tip penetration: pressure of *head* against *video tape surface*.

TIS—Travelers' Information Service: local automobilist information *transmitted* at 530 and 1650 *HKz*.

tit: in Britain, start button.

title: line(s) of descriptive information on *screen* or television *tube*. See: *drop shadow, subtitle*. Compare: *caption*.

title card: *titling* artwork for *film* or television camera photography. See: *hot press*.

tivicon: low-light camera *pickup tube* with silicon diode coated *target*.

to length: matching pre-determined *time slot*.

tolerance: acceptance limit.

tombstone: final (immobile) product layout required in all *NAB Code* toy *commercials*.

tone: pure *hue* with added black or white. Also: *1,000-Hz audio line up signal*. Also: Degree of gray mixed into pure *hue*.

tone control: electronic *circuit filter* varying *high* and *low frequency response*.

tongue: *dolly camera boom*.

top 40: popular music *radio station format*. See: *contemporary*.

top hat—high hat: *tripod* extension for high camera angles; also used by itself for low camera angles.

topless: sexually-oriented "conversation" *radio programming, FCC*-banned since 1973.

top 100: the major U.S. markets. See: *MNA*.

Toshiba: major Japanese electronics manufacturer.

total audience plan: *spot* announcement combination package designed to deliver maximum weekly *broadcast* audience.

total audience rating: number of *television homes* viewing at least six minutes of a *telecast*.

tower: loosely, *broadcast station antenna*.

tpi: (screw) threads per inch.

TPO: *transmitter signal power output*.

trace: *cathode ray tube* display created by moving *beam*.

track: *video tape* or *film audio* (*soundtrack*). Also: Camera *dolly* planks or rails. Also: Follow performer's movement with moving camera. See: *follow shot, truck*. Compare: *pan, zoom*. Also: Follow *satellite* path with *earth station antenna*.

tracking: *video tape playback-to-recording head* path match. Also: Following a *pre-recorded* path.

trade out: see *barter*.

Trades Union Congress—TUC: British labor union parent body. Compare: *AFL/CIO*.

traffic: control of *commercial production* requirements for *broadcast* advertising.

trafficking: improper sale of *FCC station allocation* during *license period*.

tranny: in Britain, pocket *radio receiver* (from *transistor*). Also: In Britain, *transparency*.

transcoding: translating *PAL* color *signals* to *SECAM* standards, or vice versa.

transducer: any device converting electrical into magnetic or mechanical energy (or vice versa).

transcription: under the *AFTRA* Code, any form of *audio* reproduction for *broadcast*. Compare: *ET*.

transfer: *film* copy of television *picture tube image*. Also: *Re-record tape signal* onto another *tape*, or onto *negative film soundtrack*. See: *optical transfer*.

transformer: *voltage-*changing device.

transient: momentary *aberrant signal* response to *input* change.

transistor: tiny *semi-conductor* device performing control and *amplification* functions of larger (obsoleted) *vacuum tube*, and capable of $1,000 \times$ *amplification;* invented 1947. See: *chip, integrated circuit, microprocessor*.

transistor radio: pocket *radio* containing *transistor*(s).

transition: *optical* or *audio effect* between *scenes* or *program* sections. Compare: *straight cut*.

translator: in difficult geographical locations, low-powered, high-altitude *FM* or television *station* receiving *broadcast signals* and re-*transmitting* them on new *frequency*.

translucent: material transmitting light but breaking up its ray structure. Compare: *transparent*.

transmission controller (coordinator): in Britain, *CCR* (*central control room*) "in charge" technician.

transmission print: see *show print*.

transmit: *broadcast* an electronic *signal*.

transmitter: specialized equipment to accomplish above.

transparency: transparent *positive still film*, usually in color.

transparent: material transmitting light without breaking up its ray structure. Compare: *translucent*.

transponder: *radar*-like *satellite signal* return equipment with 40 *MHz bandwidth* (1,200 *channels*).

transport: mechanical equipment—motor, *capstan, reel spindles* and controls—to move *tape* past *recording/playback heads*.

transverse: *quad VTR scanning*.

trapeze: device suspending *set luminaire* from overhead rope or chain.

traveler: stage curtain opening horizontally.

traveling matte: action *matte* utilizing special *film filters* and lighting. Compare: *chromakey, rotoscope*.

treads: in Britain, *set* stairs.

treatment: rough *script* outline.

treble: standard *audio frequency* range (3,500–10,000 *Hz*). Compare: *bass, mid-bass, mid-range, mid-treble*.

tree: high *spotlight* support with horizontal arm *mountings*.

triad: television *picture tube's RGB* three-color *phosphor* dot cluster.

triangle: theoretical principle of *key, back* and *fill* lighting.

triaxial: short lightweight television *cable* carrying *power* as well as *sound, video* and *control signals*. Compare: *coaxial*.

trickle charger: (*AC*) *converter* dribbling (*DC*) electrons into *storage battery*, usually over 12–14 hours.

triggyback: *time* period for three *20-second commercials* sold for (only) the price of a *one-minute spot*.

trim: unused (removed) *head* and *tail* portions of *selected film take*. Also: Change *arc carbons*.

triode: *amplifying vacuum tube* (invented as "*audion*" by *De Forest* in 1906) containing single variably-charged wire mesh *grid* controlling electron flow between *negative fila-ment (cathode)* and *positive plate*. May be used as *oscillator* to generate high frequency *AC*. Now often replaced by N-P-N or P-N-P *transistors*. Compare: *diode, pentode, te-trode*.

tripack: color *film* with three layers of *emulsion*. Compare: *bipack*.

tripod: three-legged camera support. Compare: *monopod*.

trombone: *set luminaire* support.

troposphere: atmospheric band 7 to 10 miles high, "bouncing" *UHF radio waves* (300–3,000 *MHz*) for several hundred miles. Compare: *heaviside layer, ionosphere*.

truck: extensive lateral camera *dolly* movement. Compare: *arc*.

TSA—total survey area: *ARB* audience research market classifica-tion, containing 98% of total weekly *viewers*.

T(ransmission)-stop: *aperture setting* indicating amount of light actually transmitted by *lens* after *absorption* and reflection; replaces theoretical *f-stop* system. Adjacent *T-stop* numbers double (or halve) amount of transmitted light.

tube—vacuum tube: glass-enveloped electron control-and-*amplification* device, obsoleted by *transistor*. Called *valve* in Britain. Also: **tube:** loosely, *picture tube*, or television it-self.

tubesville: (from "down the tube [drain]") disasterville.

tungsten: artificial light *filament* (3,200°*K*).

tungsten-halogen: *small, highly-efficient lamp;* tungsten *filament* in a quartz envelope filled with a halogen (see *halide*) gas.

tune: adjust *radio receiver* or *transmitter* to particular *frequency*.

tuner: *AM* or *FM receiver signal* detector. Compare: *amplifier*.

turkey: flop show.

turn fast: in Britain, operate *motion picture* camera at faster-than-normal *frame speed*, producing *"slow-motion"* effect in normal *projection*.

turn over: in Britain, camera *action cue*.

turnover: index of *reach* versus *frequency;* ratio of net un-duplicated *cumulative audience* over several periods to average audience size per period.

turn slow: in Britain, operate *motion picture* camera at slower-

·188·

than-normal *frame speed,* producing "speed-up" effect in normal *projection.*

turntable: motor- or hand-driven rotating platform; used in varying sizes for *phonograph* records, camera subjects, stagecraft, etc.

turret: old rotatable television camera *mount* holding up to 5 *lenses;* obsoleted by *zoom lens.*

turtle: three-legged floor stand for *spud.* Compare: *century stand.*

TVB—Television Bureau of Advertising: trade development organization. Compare: *BBTV, RAB.*

TVHH—television households: research estimate of number of *households* with one or more television sets.

TVQ: television performer "awareness/preference" rating, based on annual questionnaires to 1,250 U.S. sample families.

tweak (up): exactly *align* electronic equipment.

tweaker: in Britain, tiny screwdriver.

tweeter: smaller member of pair of *loudspeakers,* emphasizing *high frequencies.* Compare: *woofer.*

twenty: 20-second *commercial* message, in television *film,* offering 18 seconds of *audio.* Compare: *minute, thirty, ten.*

twofold: center-hinged *flat.*

two-shot, three-shot: two persons in frame, etc.

two-step: *phonograph disk* duplication method, using silverplate of original *acetate recording* to produce a hard mold for high quantity *vinyl pressing.* Compare: *one-step.*

two-track: see *half track.*

two-way: *cable* use for both *program transmission* and *subscriber* response to same. See: *upstream.*

Tyler mount: gyroscopically-gimballed vibration-free helicopter camera *mount.*

Type B: see *segmented.*

Type C: see *non-segmented.*

U

Uher: high-quality portable ¼" *audio tape recorder* for location *production*.

UHF—"U"—ultrahigh frequency: secondary television *broadcast band*—Channels 14 to 83—470 to 890 *megahertz*—with limited range.

UL—Underwriters' Laboratories: insurance-company-sponsored research group testing safety standards.

ulcer: in Britain, a *cookie*.

ultrasonic: above audible (20–20,000 *Hz*) range. Compare: *infrasonic, sonic*.

ultrasonic cleaner—sonic cleaner: *ultra high-frequency soundwave film* cleaning device.

U-matic: *SONY*-pioneered ¾" *video cassette recording/playback* system.

umbrella: umbrella-shaped "bounce" light reflector.

unaffiliated: non-*network broadcasting station*. Compare: *independent*.

unbalanced: *film emulsion* exposed to light of incorrect or varying *color temperature*. Compare: *color balanced*.

under: low-level *background audio*.

undercrank: operate *motion picture* camera at slower-than-normal *frame speed*, producing "speed-up" effect in normal *projection*. Called *turn slow* in Britain. Compare: *overcrank*.

underexposure: too-rapid *shutter speed* and/or insufficient *aperture* matched to *film emulsion* characteristics, resulting in undesirable "light" *negative* (or *reversal*) and "dark" *print*. Compare: *overexpose*.

underground television: see *alternative television*.

understudy: substitute performer. See: *standby*. Compare: *stand-in*.

Unilux: *motion picture strobe* light photography system.

Unisette: *BASF ¼" audio cassette*. See: *ELCASET*. Compare: *Compact*.

United Scenic Artists: scenic designers' union.

unit manager: *network* employee coordinating (among other elements) a *program's commercial* advertising material.

universe: total group of persons projected from a research sample. Also: Total possible *broadcast* audience (in U.S., 60,000,000 TV homes—in Britain, 16,000,000; 97% and 92% of all homes, respectively).

unmodulated: a medium with no *signal*. Compare: *modulate*.

up: high-level *background audio*.

up-cut: *edit* tightly.

UPI—United Press International: subscriber news service for *broadcast stations*, newspapers. Compare: *AP, Reuters*.

uplink: ground-to-*satellite transmission*.

upstage: stage area farthest from audience (or camera). Compare: *downstage*. Also: Unprofessionally overshadow a fellow performer.

upstream: reversed *cable transmission* (*subscriber* to facility). See: *up the line*.

up the line: towards *signal's* source. Compare: *down the line*.

US—naff: in Britain, useless, no good. Compare: *NG*.

use: *air* performance.

USP—unique selling proposition: putative superiority of advertised product.

V

vacuum guide: *VTR* device holding *video tape* close to *record/playback heads.*

vacuum tube—tube: glass-enveloped electronic control and *amplification* device, obsoleted by *transistor.* Designated *"V"* on *schematics.* Called *valve* in Britain.

value: color *brightness* measurement.

valve: in Britain, obsolete glass electronic control and *amplification* device. Designated *"V"* on *schematics.*

van: *remote video tape recording* truck.

vanda: (telephone company contraction) *v*ideo *and a*udio *connection.*

variable area: standard *film optical soundtrack,* utilizing variations in *modulation* width. (See below.)

variable density: alternate type of *film optical soundtrack,* utilizing variations in *modulation density.* (See above.)

variable speed motor—wild motor: *film* camera attachment permitting controlled *over-* or *under-cranking.*

"vast wasteland": epithet applied (1961) to American television *programming* by then *FCC* Chairman Newton Minow.

vault: fireproof *film* storage facility.

VCR—video cassette recorder: *video tape recorder/player* for (usually $^3/_4''$) *video cassette tapes.*

vectorscope: round (green) *oscilloscope CRT* for visual angle calibration of both *amplitude* and *phase* of the three television color signals.

velocity compensator: *video tape playback* accessory to eliminate *banding* (horizontal color *distortion*).

velour: non-reflective *drape* material, usually black.

venetian blind effect: see *hum bars*.

VERA—Vision Electronic Recording Apparatus: early (1952) *BBC b/w video recording* technique, with *tape speeds* up to 200 *ips*.

vertical interval: in Britain, brief moment, measured in *microseconds,* during which the electron *scanning beam* returns to top of television *picture tube*. See: *Ceefax, ORACLE, SLICE, Teletext, Viewdata*.

vertical interval editing: imperceptible *helical VTR editing* during *vertical blanking pulse*.

vertical interval reference—VIR: additional *signal transmitted* during *vertical blanking pulse*.

vertical interval switch: replace one *video signal* with another during *vertical blanking pulse*.

vertical resolution: number of horizontal lines in television *image*. Compare: *horizontal resolution*.

vertical retrace: see *blanking interval*.

vertical saturation: heavy *commercial scheduling* throughout *broadcast* day to reach all of *station's* audience. Compare: *roadblocking, horizontal saturation*.

VFL—variable focal length: See: *zoom lens*.

VHF—"V"—very high frequency: original television *broadcast band*—Channels 2 to 13—from 54 to 216 *megahertz*. In Britain, *frequency modulation radio broadcasting*.

video: (from Latin "see") *picture* portion of television *broadcast*. Compare: *audio*. Also: *storyboard* or *script* "pictures."

video analyzer: electro-optical device *scanning* a color *negative* to establish proper *printing exposures*. See: *Hazeltine*.

video cartridge: *Ampex* and *RCA station playback* device containing short 2″ *quad video tape* (usually a *commercial*).

video cassette: *video tape* container, usually ¾″ gauge. See: *U-Matic*.

video disk: *slow-motion* or *freeze frame* equipment (introduced in 1965). See: *slow-mo*. Also: New technique for inexpensive mass production of television *recordings*—utilizing *laser* beams, metal *styli*, etc.

video engineer—shader: technician controlling television *picture* quality (*black level, color balance, exposure gamma, video gain*) for *switcher*.

video gain: television *picture* black-to-white ratio (*contrast* control on home *receivers*).

video game: *microprocessor* attachment modifying home television *receiver* into controllable *CRT* "playing" area.

videogram: television reproduction in *cassette* or *disk* form.

video leader: standard *SMPTE* designation: :10 *color bars;* :15 *slate;* :08 *countdown;* :02 black. See: *leader*.

video looping: *video signal feed* to multiple *monitors*.

Videoplayer: Kodak device projecting *Super 8 film* into home television *receiver*.

video processing amplifier—proc amp: electronic device to alter *video signal* (*sync, picture,* color) characteristics.

video signal: electrical television *picture frequencies,* ranging from zero to approximately 4 *MHz*.

video tape: non-*sprocketed* plastic tape ¼″ to 2″ wide, coated with magnetizable metallic *oxides* to *record* (or *re-record*) television presentations. Compare: *audio tape*.

Videovoice: (*RCA*) device to transmit *slow-scanned stills* or *freeze-framed* television *pictures* over ordinary (3kHz *bandwidth*) telephone *circuits*.

vidicon: durable television camera *pickup tube* of moderate sensitivity; often used in *closed-circuit* and *film chain* operations. Compare: *image orthicon, Plumbicon, Saticon*.

Vidtronics: Technicolor *videotape-to-film transfer* system combining (3) *b/w color-separated kinescope negatives* into final color *print*. Compare: *laser*.

Viewdata: in Britain, Post Office *Teletext* application using combination of phone line *signal* plus home television *receiver*. See: *ANTIOPE*. Compare: *Ceefax, ORACLE, SLICE*.

viewer: *film editing* device. Also: Person watching television.

viewfinder: see *finder*.

viewing: *video tape playback*.

vignettes: camera shots through various-shaped opaque masks.

v.i. meter—v.u. meter: *recording level* or *volume* unit *needle*-and-dial indicator, with *decibel* scale.

(poly)vinyl(chloride)—PVC: *phonograph record pressing* material.

virgin: *tape* on which no *signal* has yet been *recorded*. Compare: *erase*.

visc: rigid home *video disk,* similar to *phonograph record*.

vision mixer: in Britain, *video switching* technician.

Visnews: international television news gathering organization.

vizmo: *rear projection* device inserting visual *backgrounds* into a *live television program*. Compare: *front projection*.

VLA—very large array: *radio* astronomy *antenna* facility.

VLF—very low frequency: *radio waves* below 30 *KHz*.

VO—voice over—off camera: television performer heard but not seen. Compare: *OC*. Called *commentary over, out-of-vision, OOV* in Britain.

VOA—Voice of America: USIA-operated *shortwave* service *transmitting* State Department *programming* (30 *transmitters* in U.S., 70 overseas).

volt—v: basic unit of *potential* difference and electromotive force. Compare: *ampere, ohm, watt*.

volume: *audio intensity*. See: *loudness*.

volume control—fader—pot: *rheostat* raising or lowering *audio* or *video levels*.

VPS—viewers per set: audience survey count of *viewers* in same household.

VTR—video tape recorder: complex electronic/mechanical device (introduced in 1956) to record *television sound* and *picture* on *magnetic tape* for instantaneous *monitor* playback. Compare: *ATR, projector, VTR*.

VTR operator: engineer handling *video tape recording*. Compare: *projectionist*.

V-2: Nazi military forerunner of USSR rocket that launched and orbited first *satellite* (*Sputnik,* 1957).

W

waiver: approved departure from standard procedure (in *production* requirements, *talent* payments, etc.)

walkie-talkie: portable *battery*-operated *wireless transmitter/receiver*.

walk-on: non-speaking performer.

walkthrough: rough *rehearsal* without cameras.

walla-walla: onomatapoeic crowd sound. See: *omnies*.

wall rack: wall-mounted *editing bin*.

WARC—World Administrative Radio Conference: international *frequency-allocation* body.

wardrobe: performers' costumes.

warm: slightly yellowish or reddish television *picture*. Compare: *cool*.

warmup: *live* introduction to *broadcast* audience prior to *air*.

waste circulation: non-potential customers exposed to television *commercial*.

water bag: water-filled heavy rubber bag to weight *set*-stand legs, etc. Compare: *sandbag*.

watt: (after the Scottish inventor) unit of electric *power* equal to one *ampere* of current under one *volt* of pressure. Wattage = *voltage* × *amperage*. Compare: *ohm*.

wave: disturbance transferring energy between adjacent particles in medium or space. Electromagnetic waves travel 3×10^{10} centimeters (186,000 miles) per second.

wave form monitor—WVFM: *oscilloscope* tube for visual analysis (and adjustment) of television *signal* characteristics.

wavefront reconstruction: (invented by Gabor in 1947) precursor of *holography*.

waveguide: straight nitrogen-filled metal pipe *transmitting* many *EHF signals* simultaneously.

wavelength: Loosely, *broadcast frequency;* measurable distance between corresponding wave points of like *phase*. Longer *wavelength* = lower *frequency*. See: *amplitude*.

wax pencil—wax crayon: see *china marker*.

weave: undesirable lateral *film* movement in *projector gate*.

web: broadcast *network*.

wedge—step wedge—step tablet: length of *motion picture negative* for *processing* control, each *frame* progressively darker. Compare: *camera test, cinex*. Also: *Test pattern* design to check camera *resolution*.

weighting: television market "point" numbers used to calculate *talent re-use* fees.

Westar: two Western Union *geosynchronous* U.S. communications *satellites* (the first launched in 1974, 22,300 miles high at 99° W.). Extensively used by *PBS* and *pay cable*. Compare: *SatCom*.

wet cell: *storage battery* requiring water for its electricity-producing chemical reaction. See: *lead acid accumulator*. Compare: *dry cell*.

wet gate—liquid gate: *printing* process placing tetrachlorethylene coating solution on *negative film* to minimize any surface defects.

"Westinghouse Rule": see *Prime Time Access Rule* (based on Westinghouse Broadcasting Company's successful petition to *FCC*).

whip (wizz) pan: in Britain, image-blurring *pan* shot, usually transitional.

white (peak) clip: automatic reduction of excessively bright television *picture* areas to correct *voltage* (1.0 *v*). See: *reference white*.

wide angle: short *focal length lens* with viewing angle over 45°.

widen: *dolly* or *zoom back* from *tight* camera position.

wide-screen: any *frame aspect ratio* between 1.33:1 and 2.66:1—but usually 2:1.

width: horizontal size of television *picture*. Compare: *height*.

wild: related elements *recorded* separately. Compare: *sync*.

wild motor—variable speed motor: camera attachment permitting controlled *over-* or *under-cranking*.

wild spot: *commercial* prepared for local *station break* use by advertiser with national or regional product distribution. Compare: *participation*.

wild track: *recording* non-*synchronized sound*.

window: margin for technical error.

windscreen—windshield: *microphone* covering. Compare: *pop filter*.

windup: talent cue to finish.

wing: perform without *rehearsal*. Compare: *block*.

wipe: *optical effect* using a line or shape to generate a new scene. Also: To *erase magnetically recorded* information.

wireless mike: performer's concealed *microphone broadcasting voice signal* directly to *receiver/recorder*. Called *radio mike* in Britain.

wireless (telegraphy): originally, *transmission* of (telegraph) *signals* through space by means of *electromagnetic waves*. Now called *radio* in in the U.S., *wireless* in Britain. See: *Morse code, radiotelegraphy*.

wire recorder: *magnetic recording* device preceding development of *audio tape recorder*.

wire service: press association *broadcast* news wire. See: *AP, Reuters, UPI*.

"woof": technician's "OK."

woofer: larger member of a pair of *loudspeakers*, emphasizing *low frequencies*. Compare: *tweeter*.

wordies: in Britain, the *script*.

worklight: permanent (relatively dim) stage or *studio set* illumination.

work picture: *picture* sequence (usually with *work track*) assembled by *film editor* for approval. See: *dirty dupe*.

work print: *editor's* rough combination of *picture* and *track.* Called *cutting copy* in Britain.

work track: *audio* sequence (usually with *work picture*) assembled by *film editor* for approval.

worldize: *play back* and *re-record background sound* (music, *effects,* etc.) *live* on *location.* Compare: *mixing studio.*

wow: slow repetitive variation in *audio tape recording* or *playback speed,* causing unacceptable *distortion.* Compare: *flutter.*

wrap: to finish—and put away equipment. Also: Contact area between *tape* and *recorder heads.*

Writers' Guild of America—WGA: authors' union, comprising two divisions: WGA-East and WGA-West.

Writers' Guild of Great Britain: authors' union.

writing speed: contact speed between *VTR head* and *tape* surface.

X–Y

xenon: quartz glass *projector lamp* containing xenon gas, offering longer life expectancy, constant *color temperature* and higher illumination efficiency.

x-ray—border: overhead *luminaire strip*.

X-sheet: *animation exposure* directions.

---

yagi: directional television *receiver antenna*.

Y & R—Young & Rubicam: major advertising agency.

yellow: subtractive element of color *negative film*. See: *cyan, magenta*.

yoke: television *scanning* and *picture tube* magnetic neck coil to coordinate *deflection* of electron stream (*beam*) from tube *gun*.

Y signal: color television *luminance signal* (4.5 *MHz*). Compare: *I signal, Q signal*.

YTV—Yorkshire: one of British *IBA's* "*Big Five*" (the *Central Companies*).

Z

Z: *impedance* symbol.

zero cutting: *negative editing* technique utilizing *A and B rolls* to hide *splice* marks.

ZDF: West Germany's nationwide "Second TV Network." Compare: *ARD*.

zip pan—swish pan: image-blurring *pan* shot, usually *transitional*. Called *flash pan* or *whip* (*wizz*) *pan* in Britain.

Zöetrope: early slotted-drum *animation* device (Horner, 1834). Compare: *Phenakistoscope, Praxinoscope*.

zonal stripe: in Britain, clear *35mm sprocketed* film with continuous ferrous *oxide* strip for *recording soundtrack*.

Zone I, I-A, II: basic *FCC FM station* operating area classifications.

zoom: alter a *lens' focal length;* a *"dolly"* without moving the camera (with no change in *parallax* conditions). Compare: *track*.

zoom lens: variable *focal length lens* (usually 10 to 1) originally designed to eliminate *lens* changing, now also used to produce the effect of rapid (or slow) camera movement towards or away from a subject. Compare: *prime lens*.

Zöopraxiscope: early "moving picture" projector (Muybridge, 1880).

Zworykin: U.S. television pioneer.